veld

THE GARDENS AND LANDSCAPES OF PATRICK WATSON

veld

THE GARDENS AND LANDSCAPES OF PATRICK WATSON

GARRETH VAN NIEKERK

PHOTOGRAPHS BY **ELSA YOUNG**

ARTWORKS BY **HEIDI FOURIE**

The author and publisher are grateful to Oppenheimer Generations Research and Conservation for its generous support towards the publication of this book.
www.ogresearchconservation.org

Published by Struik Nature
(an imprint of Penguin Random House South Africa (Pty) Ltd)
Reg. No. 1953/000441/07
The Estuaries No. 4, Oxbow Crescent,
Century Avenue, Century City, 7441
PO Box 1144, Cape Town, 8000 South Africa

Visit www.struiknature.co.za and join the Struik Nature Club for updates, news, events and special offers.

First published in 2024
10 9 8 7 6 5 4 3 2 1

Copyright © in text, 2024: Garreth van Niekerk
Copyright © in photographs, 2024: Elsa Young, unless otherwise indicated
Copyright © in paintings, 2024: Heidi Fourie
Copyright © in published edition, 2024: Penguin Random House South Africa (Pty) Ltd

Images of Stark Studios (pp. 188–195), Bobbejaanskloof (pp. 218–225) and Peninsula House (pp. 264–267) were originally published in *House & Garden* between 2013 and 2018.

Publisher: Pippa Parker
Managing editor: Roelien Theron
Project manager: Alan Hayward
Art director: Leanie Nortjé
Designers: Gillian Black, Janice Evans
Editors: Jane Carruthers, Carol Knoll
Copy editor: Gill Gordon
Proofreader: Emsie du Plessis

Reproduction by Studio Repro
Printed and bound in China by
1010 Printing International Ltd.

ISBN (Standard Edition) 978 1 7798 9021 4
ISBN (Collector's Edition) 978 1 7798 9025 2

All rights reserved. No part of this publication may be reproduced, stored in a retrieval system, or transmitted, in any form or by any means, electronic, mechanical, photocopying, recording or otherwise, without the prior written permission of the copyright owner(s).

 Making illegal copies of this publication, distributing them unlawfully or sharing them on social media without the written permission of the publisher may lead to civil claims or criminal complaints.
Protect the communities who are sustained by creativity.

For Domo,
who reminded us to be kind

CONTENTS

Author's acknowledgements — 11
Foreword — 12

GARDENS AND LANDSCAPES

1 ISIBINDI ESTATE — 23
Sandton, Johannesburg

2 SPIER ESTATE — 39
Stellenbosch, Western Cape

3 DARAHEEN FARM — 57
Tulbagh, Western Cape

4 WATERFALL ESTATE — 71
Midrand, Johannesburg

5 CAPE CLASSIC — 79
Bishopscourt, Cape Town

6 MORULENG CULTURAL PRECINCT — 91
Moruleng, North West Province

7 BIRDSVIEW ESTATE — 101
Inanda, Johannesburg

8 LOST CITY — 108
Pilanesberg, North West Province

9 NORTH ISLAND — 123
Seychelles, East Africa

10 NIROX ESTATE — 143
Cradle of Humankind, Gauteng

11 iSTORE — 174
Sandton, Johannesburg

12 THE GREENS — 179
Sandhurst, Johannesburg

13 STARK STUDIOS — 188
Randburg, Johannesburg

14
CLIVIA HOUSE 196
Khyber Rock, Johannesburg

15
GARDEN ROMANCE 204
Craighall, Johannesburg

16
27 BOXES PARK 211
Melville, Johannesburg

17
BOBBEJAANSKLOOF 219
Plettenberg Bay, Western Cape

18
STEYN CITY 226
Midrand, Johannesburg

19
ARCADIA 238
Parktown, Johannesburg

20
VICTORIA YARDS 256
Lorentzville, Johannesburg

21
PENINSULA HOUSE 264
Llandudno, Cape Town

22
SAXON HOTEL, VILLAS AND SPA 268
Sandhurst, Johannesburg

23
SCARBOROUGH HOUSE 274
Scarborough, Cape Town

PATRICK WATSON

BIOGRAPHICAL SKETCH 280
THE GARDENER'S GARDEN 290

SELECTED PLANT LISTS

PLANT LISTS 295
1. Isibindi Estate 296
2. Spier Estate 300
3. Daraheen Farm 304
4. Moruleng Cultural Precinct 308
5. North Island 310
6. Nirox Estate (Reflection) 312
7. Arcadia (The Pines) 316

REFERENCES

SELECTED REFERENCES 320

AUTHOR'S ACKNOWLEDGEMENTS

Patrick smilingly referred to himself in our first few meetings together as simply a 'gardener'. Not a landscape architect, or architect, or artist even. And so it is for this sort of audience – those passionate about design, plants, wildlife, and the art of how those exist together, whatever that may be called – that we have published this book.

As this is the first volume to explore Patrick's work, it is of course my hope that it creates some opportunity for his life and projects to be studied further, and understood for their breadth. But there are not enough pages for this author to capture the full scope of what he has accomplished over the last forty years. In trying to navigate the extent of his massive body of work, which numbers in the hundreds of gardens (completed and ongoing), we have zoomed in on the gardens that Patrick himself loosely refers to as veld gardens. If the reader is able to close the last pages and understand even the beginning of his ambitions then I, and the incredible team of people who have so lovingly poured their energy over years into this gargantuan task, would be very happy indeed.

The book has been arranged in three sections: the first takes a look at 23 of his gardens and landscapes around Africa; the next dives a little deeper into his inspiring professional and personal life; and the concluding section presents plant lists from a selection of these projects, which we hope will assist other gardeners to understand Patrick's planting schemes better, and recreate them in their own landscapes.

The publication of this book would never have been possible without the generous support of the patrons of this edition, to whom both Patrick and I are endlessly grateful. Along with the garden owners, who welcomed us so graciously into their private spaces, we also extend a heartfelt thank you, in particular, to the late Sol Kerzner, to the Roux and Walsh families, and to Oppenheimer Generations Research and Conservation – it is because of you, and those other unnamed patrons, that we were able to create this book. We know it is long overdue, but we hope it has been worth the wait. It's time South Africa, and the world, begin to learn more about this unique designer, whom I think we all believe is a national treasure.

Putting together a project like this involved a very passionate editorial team, and the support of my partner in all things, Alan Hayward, who made sure the book never lost its way, and my sister Marissa, whose careful eye transcribing the plant lists helped so immensely, and my parents, without whom this book would never have seen the light of day. Led by Jane Carruthers, whose endearing care for research and empowering young authors like myself propelled the book into a direction that makes me very proud; Vincent Carruthers, who kept us on track; Dave Kirkby, who has, over the last 40 years, maintained the records that made the research for this book possible, and shared them so kindly; and of course Keith Kirsten, who has been an extraordinary champion of this project from the outset. Carol Knoll, whose wealth of expertise about the history of landscaping in South Africa, horticultural understanding, and insight into Patrick's work in particular, so inspired my writing. Gill Gordon, thank you for bringing your extraordinary eye for detail and passion for the craft of editing to our project. Leanie Nortjé steered the art direction of this book in such a vibrant direction – no author could ask for a kinder or more tireless creative with whom to realise this project. Heidi Fourie's paintings bring the fairy tales of Patrick's fantasy works to life. Elsa Young, what you have done with the photography of Patrick's gardens has ensured that their fleeting beauty is preserved in a way few others could have achieved – it has been a true honour for Patrick and me to journey with you on this adventure.

And then, of course, to Patrick, thank you for letting me into your life, being so open with your knowledge, for entrusting me with your story, and for the laughs we've had throughout the making of your book. It is a tribute to you, and I hope that it is only the first of many books, films and gardens that will be dedicated to enriching the understanding of your work.

Garreth van Niekerk
Johannesburg 2024

FOREWORD

Patrick Watson is currently South Africa's most innovative and versatile landscape designer. Both his personality and his work defy simple categorisation because each project is utterly unique. To many, he is best known for designing extensive mega-sites such as Sun City or entire Indian Ocean islands, but he is also the creator of exquisite small gardens at private homes, quirky witticisms like 27 Boxes Park in Melville, or quiet spaces for reflection and contemplation, such as at the Apartheid Museum in Johannesburg or the Garden of Hope at St George's Anglican Church in Parktown. Across this broad spectrum of diversity, he combines artistic intuition with extensive botanical knowledge and a deep concern for the conservation and restoration of nature. Into every project, large or small, he weaves together the potential of the natural environment, the purpose of the garden, the clients' aspirations (sometimes not fully articulated, even to themselves) and his own, often unconventional, perspective. Each project receives its own distinctive interpretation so that his gardens and landscapes are not identifiable by any recognisable 'Watson style' or template, but rather by their absolute individuality.

THE ECOLOGIST

Professionally, Patrick is a self-taught ecologist with an extensive knowledge of plants, horticulture and ecosystems. Encouraged by his supportive parents, for they too were gardeners, architects and naturalists, he has always been interested in the natural environment around him. He explains elsewhere in this book that he cannot recall a time when he was not absorbed by plants, their names, shapes, colours, growth forms and habitats. From his teenage years, he has familiarised himself with a variety of environments in many places, identifying plants, studying their growth habits, noting their ecological niches and plant communities. Remarkably, he can recall almost every one of the countless species he has encountered in his life. He is familiar with every region of South Africa – its geology, botany, climate, hydrology, soil types – and even applied a sound knowledge of palaeobotany when designing the unusual garden for the Origins Centre at the University of the Witwatersrand. Incessantly travelling, in South Africa and elsewhere, he has pioneered the propagation and cultivation of many rare species previously known only in their natural habitats. In addition, with 'green fingers', he has established viable nurseries from seed and transplanted tens of thousands of large trees into the landscapes that he has created. Nevertheless, he remains enthralled by an unspoilt landscape. The floral abundance of the Northern Cape, the majesty of ancient baobabs, the renosterveld, and the forests of Central Africa, all command his constant admiration. He believes his obsession with nature is subconscious and inborn, perhaps even genetic, inherited from an ancestral lineage that includes many men and women who were plant collectors, horticulturalists, naturalists and nurserymen.

Patrick entered his profession on the cusp of the Green Revolution of the late 1960s and early 1970s and was influenced by the ideas of Ian McHarg, the Scottish-born head of the Department of Landscape Design at the University of Pennsylvania and the author of *Design with Nature* (1969). At the time, the first photographs of Earth taken from space were appearing and Patrick was influenced by the planetary consequences of environmental change. In his work, he has a unique ability to understand the broader environment within the confines of a garden, and is able to combine these insights with his extraordinary knowledge of natural ecosystems and apply them philosophically. In every project that he tackles, there is both a strong environmental ethic and an ecological approach, and these are combined with a love of South Africa's natural beauty. Many of his more recent projects tend to include ecological restoration, creating and rebuilding lost or degraded biodiversity. His work at Steyn City is one example, and projects in Mauritius and the Seychelles are others. In the future, he may be most celebrated and esteemed for those of his plantings and designs that have re-established ecological systems and networks. He refers to these as his 'legacy projects'.

As we move further into the Anthropocene (the current epoch, in which humanity's impact on the planet includes global warming, mass extinctions, countless species relocations and the rapid global transmission of diseases), Patrick's 'legacy projects' herald an innovation in landscape design in which we think in planetary terms and in which local plants, natural resilience and ecosystems are appropriate and sustainable. Such projects signal a unity of humans with nature, raise levels of awareness, nurture the biosphere, and promote a conservation ethic. Those who are aware of his considerable botanical knowledge and ecological sensitivity regard these qualities as an important reason for his success.

THE ARTIST

One may describe Patrick as a landscape architect, botanist, horticulturalist, or ecologist, but, in essence, he is an artist. His projects are creative, fresh with inspiration, often bold, never derivative. He uses plants, colours, landform and space as a painter or sculptor might work with oils, canvas, or bronze, and from them he creates visual and emotional experiences. He has an extraordinary ability to exploit his medium to the full, blending plants and place to bring forth a living scenescape of joy and interest.[1]

As an artist, his talent is innate and intuitive; once his ideas and concepts begin to germinate, they demand the freedom to express themselves and evolve creatively. He has described his ideas for any project as a combination of insight and flashes of inspiration. However, Patrick has a talent not commonly shared by artists in paint or marble. He is able to visualise how his projects will develop long into the future. Gardens and landscapes are living organisms that change and evolve over time, and the landscapes he designs take account of that process and continue to transform and benefit from it. It is this skill of anticipating what his creation will look like long after he has gone that makes his work so unusual. Lancelot 'Capability' Brown, possibly England's most creative landscaper, who revolutionised the image of the English countryside into the form that much of it exists to this day, also had the ability to foresee the appearance of a planted landscape after the passage of decades. However, for all his genius, Brown had a recognisable 'style' and styles can be replicated even after the hand of the master has been removed.

Patrick is no follower of any school, although he is knowledgeable of garden fashions both historical and current. His gardens cannot be duplicated. In this, he is more like the Australian gardener Edna Walling,[2] producing a kind of music or poetry with what is created out of plants and soil, a harmony for the eyes, for the mind and for the spirit – a true art form that demands an emotional response.

Patrick does not work to templates, he is not a linear-thinking engineer or technician, restricted by unalterable designs, budgets or imposed ideology. He finds rules formulated by others extremely limiting to his mind and imagination and has said that formal education, even in the landscape field, may stifle creativity rather than nurture it.

---

1 Karyn Richards, 'Profile on Patrick Watson', *Landscape SA*, November 2006.

2 Peter Watts, *Edna Walling and her Gardens*. Balmain Sydney: Florilegium, 1991, pp. 9–11.

He prefers to follow nature. As an artist he is original, idiosyncratic, flexible, and truly visionary, planting without any seeming order while creating a whole.

Unlike many other talented South African landscape designers, such as Joane Pim or Ann Sutton, who left extensive archives of plans and correspondence, Patrick has no drafting office or secretarial staff to assist him. He works mainly without drawings, precise specifications, or bills of quantities. Unless the project is formal and geometric, all the planning takes place in his mind, for he can internally comprehend the scale (no matter how extensive) and every aspect of what he aims to achieve for his client. Watson's archives are his gardens. He has been fortunate to work with contractors, like Dave Kirkby of Top Turf, who have been able to translate his sometimes vague, handwritten lists, rough sketches and visual ideas into usable data, budgets and quantities. Kirkby was energised and inspired by Patrick, relishing the rich conversations and intensive research that went into the start of every project. Kirkby also appreciated that working for Patrick Watson, unlike other landscape designers and architects, had no routine. Instead, as he attested, it came with 'the stimulation of pushing the boundaries of complexity… coming up with projects which inspired me rather than overawed me.'[3]

THE PHILOSOPHER

Patrick's artistic approach sometimes obscures the fact that he is a serious philosopher who often uses the word 'philosophy' to explain the purpose of his work. What he achieves with plants and space is never flippant or merely an attractive diversion. Recognising that a garden is a living process, very often of great importance to a client, he knows that he needs to create a landscape that is in tune with the client's philosophy without compromising his own. Plants matter, as does the environment that nurtures them. As an ecologist, he appreciates that plants are significant in themselves, they are a functional part of the biosphere and not mere toys or decorations to be played with by humans for their amusement. Being a plant philosopher is a solemn endeavour, requiring gravitas, as he expresses it. He knows that his decisions have long-term consequences and must be carefully contemplated, defensible, measured, and executed without egotism or vanity. Whatever he does, however contentious it might be, it must be wise, and able to stand the test of time.

His art is a long-term environmental commitment. Moreover, whatever he is engaged in must be authentic, without pretence or facade. Certainly, he has, in the course of his career, created fantasies, and he enjoys the fact that his creations are sometimes controversial and provoke discussion and debate. But his theatrical creations, like the Lost City, are intended to be make-believe fantasy and enjoyed as such, not as a parody or pastiche of nature.

THE PROFESSIONAL

At first meeting, Patrick may come across as eccentric, shy and rather quietly spoken, although he is a good conversationalist when he chooses to be. One soon learns, however, that he is always approachable and never reticent to explain himself, his work, or his ideas.

Gardening at every scale, large or small, is a collaborative endeavour and Patrick is well known in the industry for his integrity and uncompromising intolerance of imperfection. Based on these principles, he has built long-lasting relationships with clients, contractors, horticulturalists and landscapers. One of his little-known, but most important, contributions to the industry has been the training and empowering of several nurserymen and gardeners. His guidance and support have launched them on successful careers of their own. Valuing teamwork, he listens to suggestions and welcomes brainstorming. Constantly adventurous, his reaction to fresh ideas and opportunities is invariably to respond, with a wry smile, 'Why not?'

Relationships with clients are particularly important in this business and Patrick is well skilled in this regard. He holds firm opinions, and trusts completely in his own judgement, talents and decisions, but he is never strident or dogmatic in expressing his views.

Over the years, he has collaborated with numerous clients. They have varied from powerful personalities with abundant means and extensive properties to others with small spaces, leaner finances and more idiosyncratic personal tastes. Many are eccentric, with formidable reputations and commensurate egos, but his quiet, quirky manner invariably wins them over. He first listens to his clients and their ideas and gains their confidence, and then creates something unique. He has the imagination to appreciate the possibilities that each site possesses, possibilities that may emerge as astounding surprises that delight and might never have been anticipated. Very occasionally, a client has found his unusual manner difficult, but none can deny the sincerity of his well-informed opinions and the consistency of his success.

---

3 Dave Kirkby, *Stars, Blinks and Dots (and a Little Chutzpah)*. Johannesburg: Beyond the Vale Publishing, 2012, pp. 166–167.

ABOVE In conceptualising the gardens for the Apartheid Museum in Ormonde, to the south of Johannesburg, Patrick looked to Highveld landscapes, working with indigenous veld species and forms inspired by the architecture of this historic museum, where entrances and pathways separate visitors according to their own choices. A journey through the museum can be an emotional one, but the gardens offer a tranquil space for reflection. (*Images courtesy Apartheid Museum*)

THE TRIBUTE

My husband, Vincent, and I have known Patrick for more than five decades and have been fortunate to be exposed to his enormous creativity, wide knowledge, generosity and kindness. He is extraordinarily well read, thoughtful and highly observant. It has been a pleasure for us, and for many of his friends, to have watched the unfolding of his remarkable career, the execution of his ideas, the impact they have had and the acclaim he has received.

Despite his lack of formal qualification, Patrick has been recognised by his peers. His career began at a time when the landscape design community in South Africa was professionalising and he attended early conferences and meetings of the Institute for Landscape Architecture in South Africa and worked with some of its founders. He is currently an honorary member and, in 2017, was the recipient of the Institute's Lifetime Award.

Patrick Watson's combination of talents is extremely rare. He is a free spirit whose work is always fresh, inspiring and interesting. He is a truly original South African artist, whose lasting legacy will be in his having united humanity and the natural world in a deeper understanding through the variety and power of his landscape art.

The publication of *Veld: The Gardens and Landscapes of Patrick Watson* is a superb tribute to an extraordinary person. It is a recognition of the remarkable combination of knowledge, skill and instinct that is the complex Patrick Watson, and the radical influence that he has had on his profession.

Jane Carruthers
Environmental Historian
Emeritus Professor Unisa
Johannesburg 2024

THIS SPREAD Jane and Vincent Carruthers in their tranquil Johannesburg garden, designed by Patrick to provide a natural haven for suburban wildlife, particularly the many frogs that make their home in the pond and adjacent aquatic habitat. (*Images courtesy Keith Kirsten Horticulture*)

GARDENS AND LANDSCAPES

1
ISIBINDI ESTATE
Sandton, Johannesburg

Grassland • Horizon • Meadow

In the heart of Johannesburg's new Central Business District, the Highveld – that quintessentially South African landscape spread across the country's central plateau – has inspired Patrick's design of three interwoven gardens set within a historical private estate. Commissioned between 2003 and 2005, the gardens explore naturalistic planting inspired, and then abstracted, by various Highveld habitats. At its root, Isibindi is about seeing veld plants in all their splendour, across every season, and paying tribute to the owner's family legacy of indigenous gardening and commitment to conservation.

LEFT Early morning mist falls across Isibindi's meadowland, with its masses of herbaceous flowering species, where the canopies of two Paperbark Thorn Trees (*Vachellia sieberiana* var. *woodii*) reach towards each other.

Bulbous plants, such as species of *Chlorophytum*, *Agapanthus* and *Eucomis*, grow beneath the Paperbarks (*Vachellia* spp.) in the garden's Highveld-inspired meadow.

NEARLY TWO DECADES HAVE PASSED since Patrick's initial design work on Isibindi Estate. His continued sourcing of plants for the designs, maintained by a resident team of horticultural staff, has seen the original parkland design (which dates back to the 1930s) now seamlessly incorporating a contemporary Highveld meadow, grassland and wetland. Each landscape celebrates unique aspects of Highveld habitats, while also acknowledging the estate's history.

Patrick's work began with the establishment of a large artificial clay catchment pond and grass berm at the lowest end of the site, accessed by a low-slung timber suspension bridge, hanging in parts on the water's surface. Since the plants have established themselves, the area has grown into a lush indigenous wetland surrounded by swaying emergent Wetland Grass (*Eleocharis dregeana*) and African Bulrush (*Typha capensis*). The pond is full of the floating aquatic Blue Water Lily (*Nymphaea nouchali* var. *caerulea*), its spongy roots now firmly anchored in the pan and its lavender, sky-blue and pale pink flowers jostling among the roving wild ducks. The rare Arum (*Zantedeschia albomaculata*), salvaged by Patrick and the team from civil infrastructural developments that were encroaching on a wetland nearby, grow on the pond's embankments alongside masses of the marsh-loving *Eulophia welwitschii* orchid, known as 'umlunge' in isiZulu, whose pale yellow flowers with dark purple centres come up following the summer rains. Varied shades of pink from the threatened Wetland Orchid (*Satyrium hallackii*), which has two subspecies, also enliven the wetland landscape, to be joined later in the season by the inflorescences, red in bud and greenish white when mature, of Torch Lily (*Kniphofia ensifolia*). The smaller *K. porphyrantha* appears in summer. Its buds are orange, but the open flowers turn a distinctive lemon-yellow, indicating that they have been pollinated by insects. The triangular spikes provide perfect perches for the brightly coloured male Southern Red Bishop, with its harems and its woven nests in the reed beds around the wetland.

The footbridge traverses on one side into a curvaceous lawn, at first hidden behind swaying masses of large, creamy-white plumes of Bush Grass (*Calamagrostis epigejos*) at the start of the Highveld grassland area of the garden. The browns, pinks and mauves of other indigenous low-growing grasses have been planted on extraordinarily large scales across this section, creating differing heights beside the mown lawn and establishing what Patrick describes as 'the emotion of an endless horizon'. The mass grass planting also sets a plain canvas for the seasonal flowering of occasional veld flowers, such as the spring-flowering scarlet flower spikes of the locally indigenous deciduous *Erythrina zeyheri*, an intriguing dwarf shrub of the high plateau. The huge underground stem of this plant produces large leaves with curved prickles, offering protection against herbivores. The pendulous lily-like, pink Orange River Lily (*Crinum bulbispermum*) grows among the erythrinas. The grasses die off almost completely in winter, giving the owners the opportunity every few years to set the grassland on fire, revealing in the afterburn the vivid greens of fresh grass and fire-dependent flowers in the blackened earth, as nature intended.

Across the footbridge, a path of roughly hewn stones takes one into the heart of the garden's Highveld meadow. Emerging from behind the branches of the estate's youngest

> "Across the escarpment there are these deep, flat grasslands that seem to go on forever and, aesthetically, in this garden, I wanted to communicate that sensation of an endless African horizon."

Paperbark Thorn (*Vachellia sieberiana* var. *woodii*), an open field of low-lying herbaceous perennials comes into full view, ablaze with colour, texture and the sounds of insects – a rarity in Johannesburg's suburbia. Planted along geometric and symmetrical paths, it is remarkable that almost 600 different species of low-growing perennials flourish abundantly here.

Patrick's mass planting in this area works towards a careful choreography of seasonal colour. A sea of yellow comes in spring from groups of the bristly *Berkheya* species, early flowering species of *Gazania*, *Helichrysum*, *Senecio* and hairy-leaved *Hypoxis* species. Thereafter come waves of purple-blue in summer from clumps of agapanthus, compact bushes of wild Michaelmas Daisy (*Felicia erigeroides*), with their fragile, pale mauve flowers, and Blue Stars (*Aristea ecklonii*). Drooping Agapanthus (*Agapanthus inapertus*) add a touch of pale blue and purple alongside the bright deciduous Bell Agapanthus or Bloulelie (*A. campanulatus*). Plentiful purples continue from species such as Vernonia (*Hilliardiella oligocephala*), between which the ivory blooms of Grass Vlei Lily (*Crinum graminicola*) appear in late spring.

The meadow thereafter bursts into vibrant greens and pale creamy-whites with fragrant tendrils of African Wormwood (*Artemisia afra*) and the tall flower stems of *Chlorophytum bowkeri*, a favourite of the carpenter bee with its 'buzz pollination' that shakes loose the pollen of this plant onto its hairy back. Also flowering at this time is *Cephalaria zeyheriana*, with its dome-shaped white flowerhead being a particular favourite of honeybees. Tufts of the leaf-like rosette of *Eucomis autumnalis* – a longer-leaved, darker green variety of the Pineapple Lily – bring interest and focus to this now emerald summer pasture. Smaller flowering plants such as *Hibiscus aethiopicus*, Doll's Protea (*Macledium zeyheri*) and Chocolate Bells (*Trichodesma physaloides*), with its drooping blooms and turquoise leaves, have been planted close to the edges of the paths so that their inconspicuous beauty can be appreciated.

Moving away from the estate's original English parkland aesthetic of lawns and clustered groups of trees, Patrick turned for inspiration to the Dutch botanical still life paintings of the 17th century. The Cape Dutch architecture of the main residence required a connection to the landscape and, for Patrick, the unique focus on individual wildflowers in traditional Dutch still life art was closer to the client's brief that sought a more 'delicate and detailed' garden than the expansive grasslands or parks across the rest of the estate.

ABOVE The meadowlands comprise a colourful display of daisy species, including this fragile wild Michaelmas Daisy (*Felicia erigeroides*).

FOLLOWING SPREAD Viewed from above, the geometry of the grass paths in the Highveld meadow is revealed, showing how they intersect between a series of triangular beds brimming with veld species, many of them salvaged from construction sites in the surrounding areas.

ABOVE The planting programme looks to the Cape Dutch-inspired architecture of the home by referencing Dutch still life paintings of the 17th century, which were celebrated for their focus on flowers and the importance of the detail of each specimen.

OPPOSITE Hundreds of Pineapple Lily (*Eucomis autumnalis*) flower from midsummer.

Each space invites one to appreciate it fully, immersing oneself deeply in their wild dissimilitude. Whether viewed from bridges or paths, the landscapes are designed to surround and allow a momentary escape from the energy of the city on the doorstep. As Johannesburg spreads, there will be fewer sanctuaries such as this in which wildlife can find a home.

These gardens are alive with birdlife and abuzz with insects, and are an excellent example of how a commitment to restoring private gardens can uplift the wider urban ecology. In sharing this project, the owners and Patrick have made an effort to take urban conservation further by attempting, wherever possible, to gather plants from construction sites nearby, where vital habitats are destroyed almost every day. Sadly, success does not always come easily. At most, Patrick and his team are able to save around five percent of what they collect from these development sites. Isibindi has also made significant efforts to save water by ensuring that only newly transplanted plants are artificially watered, typically by hand, with the remainder of the gardens relying on Johannesburg's seasonal rains.

Patrick continually finds unusual specimens to add to the growing miscellany of plants in these gardens, and is working towards expanding a small indigenous forest into the wetland area.

Formal pathways intersect with wild plantings at the centre of Patrick's unique layout of the meadowland at Isibindi. The lawn paths are steel-edged to contain their growth, allowing native species to grow abundantly in the adjacent areas and also to attract a variety of insects and birds.

ABOVE A footbridge crosses over a clay catchment pond in the wetland section of the garden, where aquatic species such as African Bulrush (*Typha capensis*) and Blue Water Lily (*Nymphaea nouchali* var. *caerulea*) attract visiting birdlife and amphibians.

OPPOSITE Grass stairs cut out of the lawns themselves connect the residence to the front garden and Highveld meadow beyond.

> "I tried to make the garden into one big space, so you can see from one end of the garden to the other, and really appreciate the scale in the middle of suburbia. I also wanted to communicate the genius of the Highveld, which is mesmerising."

ABOVE AND OPPOSITE A multitude of birds and wildlife have found sanctuary between the verdant aquatic vegetation that grows at the water's edge and, beyond its surface, in the garden's wetland.

LEFT AND ABOVE Once a year, the grasslands of Isibindi Estate erupt in breathtaking bursts of scarlet and dusty pink from the inflorescences and umbels of Plough-breaker (*Erythrina zeyheri*) and Orange River Lily (*Crinum bulbispermum*).

2
SPIER ESTATE
Stellenbosch, Western Cape

Fields • Fynbos • Flair

Established in 1692, the Spier Estate in the Stellenbosch region of the Western Cape is one of the oldest wine farms in South Africa. It is celebrated as much for its wine, fruit, grain crops and livestock as it is for its cultural significance and splendid floriculture. One of the Cape's most popular tourist destinations, the estate is visited by over a million guests, conference delegates, vintners and pleasure-seekers each year.

FOR THE PAST TWO DECADES, Patrick has led a large-scale restoration and conservation programme across Spier's vast 650 hectares. Working alongside head gardener, Wilton Sikhosana, and within Spier's forward-looking conservation vision, Patrick has sought to create sustainable connections between the historical landscape and the unique indigenous species. In early spring, for instance, near the front of the property, thousands of lustrous, scarlet flowers burst into bloom on over 800 Coral Trees (*Erythrina lysistemon*), some of which line the avenues that lead from the hotel to its restaurants. The erythrina, among the first indigenous South African trees to be grown domestically, eloquently frames a narrative told along the path that Spier calls its Heritage Walk. The walking route takes visitors through more than three centuries of South Africa's past, telling the story by means of a series of monumental sculptures by local contemporary artists. Located here and there among the sculptures are botanical signboards that explain details of the ecological restoration that Spier has undertaken – an ongoing initiative that is full of inspiration for any gardener.

Once spelt 'Speir', the estate has had a number of owners since it was established, each of whom had left their own mark on the property. But the changing hands have wrought radical alterations to the landscape which, by the time the current owners of Spier took over the reins, had become severely degraded. As on many of the neighbouring estates, much of the locally indigenous vegetation had been lost over time to farming, and large tracts of the countryside had become overrun by invasive species. Australian Blue Gums (*Eucalyptus* spp.) and Wattles (*Acacia* spp.) had begun to suffocate the waterways, and the immensely rich local vegetation, fynbos and renosterveld, was slowly being destroyed in its natural habitat.

Restoration of the waterways became a priority of the project in its early stages, starting with the banks of the Eerste River which flows through the farm, as well as two of its tributaries, the Blaauwklippen and Bonte rivers. Patrick recognised the future crisis that the farm would face without an adequate water supply, and the practical outcome of the conservation and rehabilitation effort became crucial in realising the ambition of the project to conserve water. Within a few years, this 74-hectare riparian woodland had become an immensely powerful and dynamic biofilter that, since being stripped of its invasive vegetation, is now the lifeblood of the estate.

Today, as a result of these efforts, the banks of Spier's river grow rich with unique riverine vegetation such as the protected Breede River Yellowwood (*Podocarpus elongatus*). The fragile, open-crowned Cape Willow (*Salix mucronata*) now also grows close to the water's edge, as does the Wild Peach (*Kiggelaria africana*) with its split pods and bright orange arils, which attract fruit-eating birds to the riverside.

OPPOSITE Thousands of agapanthus planted by Patrick and Wilton Sikhosana, Spier's head gardener, flower en masse in the fields of the Spier Estate, where indigenous plantings have naturalised and restored the degraded former farmlands.

ABOVE Unique art installations by leading South African artists, like 'Bergson's Cycle' by Lyall Sprong (pictured), frame moments in the landscape. This work, as well as several others, forms part of the Spier Art Collection. Spier also facilitates the training of artists and artisans through the work of the Spier Arts Trust.

OPPOSITE Dense clusters of the white form of *Agapanthus praecox* flower between the grasses in the veld.

Alongside the river, visitors amble through a collection of some of the country's most beloved species of *Protea*, including the Sugarbush (*Protea repens*), which legend claims was the first Cape protea to have flowered in cultivation. The winter-flowering Burchell's Sugarbush (*Protea burchellii*) and clusters of Green Sugarbush (*Protea coronata*) flower along this walk, as well as a 'silver forest' of endangered Silver Trees (*Leucadendron argenteum*). This leucadendron, with its shimmering silvery haired leaves, seldom lives longer than 20 years and is locally indigenous to only a small area of the Western Cape. These softwood trees are easily felled and burnt, and also often infected by a root fungus that is leaving naturally occurring populations in outlying areas in danger of extinction.

Throughout the site, hard landscaping interventions, such as terraformed earth mounds that are set into the expansive parkland areas, appear natural, fading gently into the undulating landscape. Beyond the river, the level of an existing lake has been lowered significantly by the horticultural team, while indigenous water plants like the Blue Water Lily (*Nymphaea nouchali* var. *caerulea*), Cape Arums (*Zantedeschia aethiopica*), Floating Hearts (*Nymphoides thunbergiana*) and Waterblommetjies, also known as Cape Pond Weed (*Aponogeton distachyos*) have been introduced into the lake and other ponds. The lake's water level is now low enough to attract the quaint African Spoonbill, whose short legs and squat feet require shallow water in which to land. Visitors can watch from a distance as the colony of spoonbills nests on stick platforms in the willow trees that overhang the lake, or feeds on invertebrates among the restios that are indigenous to the Cape.

To connect the past with the estate's new future, Patrick looked not only to the vegetation of the larger property but also to what would be appropriate to the original architecture of the buildings that date from the Dutch colonial period of the Cape's history. Patrick's focus was to pare back any inappropriate plants that were not emblematic of 17th century landscaping and to remove the vines that had crept up the facades of the Cape Dutch buildings – indeed anything that more closely resembled the English romantic gardens of a later era rather than Dutch formalism.

The ancient oak trees, some more than 250 years old, on the 'werf' (homestead and farmyard) lawn, which can be seen from the restaurants and serves as a playground for younger visitors, presented another opportunity to excavate the history of this remarkable place. In order to create more spaces for play, Patrick used intense earthworks to lower the level of the lawn, revealing the edges of sculptural granite boulders that further expose the scale of the monumental oak trees.

The property's original canals have also been restored, with more of them added to channel the river water around the property. The new channels were all constructed in the same traditional way as the estate's surviving historical *grachts*, and appear as though they have always been there.

However, while the restoration of the public side of Spier Estate has been extremely significant, the full extent of Patrick and Wilton's vision is experienced in the restoration and conservation work they have undertaken in the grasslands situated at the more private end of the estate proper. Easily visited via a bridge from the werf, visitors enjoy a remarkable environmental experience where many kilometres of grasslands, fynbos and highly endangered renosterveld appear to grow wild.

Renosterveld vegetation, together with fynbos and succulent karoo, forms part of the Cape Floristic Region – the only region of the Cape Floristic Kingdom. It is the smallest of the world's six floristic kingdoms but the most diverse, consisting of more than 9,500 species of plants. Yet, where once the lowlands of the Western Cape abounded with renosterveld, today commercial fields of wheat, barley, grapes and canola have left as little as three percent of the original renosterveld intact. At Spier, remnants of this now highly endangered vegetation survive, as do portions of the smaller, perhaps even rarer, Lourensford Alluvium Fynbos and Ferricrete Fynbos, offering visitors and researchers an unprecedented glimpse into what the area may have looked like many centuries ago.

BELOW The waxy, deep blue perianth of Cape Agapanthus or Fynbos Agapanthus (*Agapanthus praecox*), which flowers in the late summer months.

OPPOSITE The scale of agapanthus planting becomes clear from above, where they flower profusely between the contemporary sculptures that line the Spier Art Walk.

To encourage access to and engagement with the veld restoration by guests, Spier has created bicycle and walking paths that wind between fields high with dense tufts of Rooigras (Themeda triandra), a grass species that was almost completely erased from the landscape by overgrazing. In early summer, the grass comes alive with masses of orange and red inflorescent spikes of Red-hot Poker or Torch Lily (Kniphofia uvaria), as well as the paler yellow and cream inflorescences of bulbinella. Between the flowering spikes, the watsonias and gladioli from last spring remain; their colourful tubes of fuchsia, magenta, tangerine and mauve just visible as the wind moves through the grasses.

One of the highlights of Spier is when summer draws to its end, and the tall, extravagant swathes of indigo, lilac and white agapanthus flowers are displayed throughout the veld and alongside buildings. The agapanthus are not all wild to the area, occurring more naturally in the Eastern Cape but, as Patrick explains, they have been introduced to bring some energy into the landscape, and add a last note of colour before autumn. Cape Agapanthus or Fynbos Agapanthus (Agapanthus praecox), which occurs naturally from the coast to about 1,200 metres above sea level, is the most common, planted closely in packed sheathes. The genus Agapanthus is locally indigenous to southern Africa and is distributed from the Cape Peninsula to the southern slopes of the mountain ranges in Limpopo. This genus occurs naturally nowhere else on Earth but is grown commercially, for floriculture and gardening, in many parts of the globe.

When autumn finally comes around, converting the landscape into sombre browns, golds and oranges, Spier is once again enlivened by an extraordinary collection of Amaryllidaceae plants, from the pale pinks of the March Lily (Amaryllis belladonna) to warm reds from spectacular clumps of nerines, and exuberant fuchsia-coloured brunsvigias.

The work of both Patrick and Wilton enables visitors to appreciate the authentic feeling of Spier's legacy, blurring the lines between the old and the new, and subtly contrasting the wild with the structured. As it evolves, the vision for the Spier landscape is becoming more confidently adventurous, with many nurserymen now dedicated to expanding the already impressive biodiversity on the site by working both with nature and the local community in innovative ways. Spier's inspiring Tree-preneur programme, which rewards community members with payment or goods, such as bicycles, for growing trees from seed for Spier, is the sort of undertaking that has seen the project awarded 'Conservation Champion' status by the World Wide Fund for Nature, among other accolades, and creates the outlines of an ethos for historic garden preservation in South Africa that is firmly grounded in expanding environmental stewardship for South Africans into the future.

OPPOSITE AND ABOVE A bridge connecting the hospitality side of the Spier Estate to the restored veld passes over the Eerste River, a dynamic biofilter that has been restored by Patrick and the Spier team.

BELOW The coral-coloured blooms of the Coral Tree (*Erythrina lysistemon*) flower annually in a magnificent display across the estate.

"I want it to be a spectacle of colour, almost like Namaqualand, with vast sheets of bulbs that change colours with the seasons."

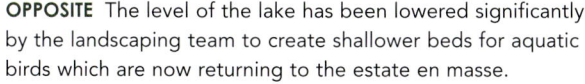

OPPOSITE The level of the lake has been lowered significantly by the landscaping team to create shallower beds for aquatic birds which are now returning to the estate en masse.

TOP Red-hot Poker (*Kniphofia uvaria*) flowers in clusters among the tall veld grasses in midsummer.

ABOVE AND RIGHT Hundreds of Coral Trees (*Erythrina lysistemon*) provide a burst of scarlet along the Heritage Walk.

From above, the enormous extent of the Spier landscape becomes clear, dominated by the new form of the lowered and expanded lake, the coral tree-lined heritage walk, and the immense veld restoration area to the far left of the image.

OPPOSITE AND ABOVE The white form of *Agapanthus praecox*, planted en masse alongside the cobbled alleys between Spier's restored Cape Dutch buildings, flowers in an extraordinary display throughout the summer months.

FOLLOWING SPREAD Agapanthus, proteas, leucadendrons, watsonias and wild grasses have been planted between works from the Spier Art Collection, such as Bronwyn Lace's 'Ourobouros' sculpture (shown here), created from the skeleton of a female rhinoceros.

OPPOSITE AND TOP Spier head gardener, Wilton Sikhosana, in the nursery, which was established over the course of a decade to supply the vast estate with plants from throughout the region.

ABOVE AND RIGHT Seeds, like these from Arum Lilies (*Zantedeschia aethiopica*), are sustainably gathered from populations of plants self-seeding across the estate.

Spier Estate

3
DARAHEEN FARM
Tulbagh, Western Cape
Renosterveld • Ecotonal • Matrix

A former agricultural site, once comprising only cultivated fields and cattle herds, has found new life in the lowlands of the Tulbagh valley. Here, local indigenous plants, some vulnerable to extinction, have reconnected the farm's homestead to the surrounding Tulbagh Breede Shale Renosterveld ecosystem. Moreover, around 46 threatened fragments of the renosterveld, incorporating some rare plant populations, have been conserved – adding further diversity to this important part of the Cape Floristic Region.

THE GARDENS OF THIS 24-HECTARE PROPERTY were commissioned by a keen environmentalist, bird enthusiast, and plant collector, for his new residence. In the past, Patrick has created several other residential gardens in farming areas, all with the brief to restore the natural landscape, and fashion a sanctuary for the families who reside there.

OPPOSITE AND ABOVE Patrick and the team who worked on this extraordinary garden undertook a 750-metre-long restoration of the riverine vegetation along the banks of the Breede River, including the reintroduction and restoration of species such as Wild Peach (*Kiggelaria africana*), Wild Olive (*Olea europaea* subsp. *cuspidata*) and Cape Holly (*Ilex mitis*).

LEFT AND ABOVE Extensive restoration of the areas surrounding Daraheen's interconnected riverbeds and lakes has ensured the return of birds and local wildlife to the area, diversifying local plant life in the process.

Patrick's work at Daraheen began when the main residence was being built. At the time, it was surrounded by weeds that remained from its previous life as a wheat field. A wildfire swept through the site in 2012, destroying the vegetation along a river that flows through the property and leaving the new house exposed to the elements. However, while the fire was destructive, it revealed the alien acacias, eucalyptus, pines and other invasive species that had overtaken the property's rivers and waterways. Black Wattles (*Acacia mearnsii*) and Port Jacksons (*A. saligna*) were felled and treated with herbicides. An indigenous seed mix, approved by Patrick, was then sown. This was followed by Patrick casting coloured-coded 'sticks' across the river system to mark where indigenous trees would be planted based on where each stick landed – a technique he has employed across the continent to simulate the patterns of natural forest growth.

By May 2014, over 11,000 trees, shrubs, grasses and bulbs had been planted along the 750 metres of riverbanks. The garden plant selection was based on the vegetation found in the undisturbed forests of the Tulbagh valley, including trees such as Wild Olive (*Olea europaea* subsp. *cuspidata*), Wild Peach (*Kiggelaria africana*), the small Breede River Yellowwood (*Podocarpus elongatus*), Cape Holly (*Ilex mitis*) and the fragile Cape Willow (*Salix mucronata*).

To create a sense of intimacy on the exposed site, protect it and connect it to the residence's courtyard-based architecture, a rectangular 'courtyard' of lawn was sown. Perennial beds were planted alongside this lawn, and edited over time, to create self-sustaining wildflower plant matrices that are diverse, resist invasion by weeds, and self-renew.

The garden beds also work to reinterpret the unique floral profile of the site by focusing on 'garden-type' species from the area. The plant list that was developed exclusively for this garden was crafted in close partnership with Tulbagh-based nurseryman and conservationist Johann van Biljon of Intaba Environmental Services. Van Biljon set up his nursery alongside his own farmhouse nearby and cultivated what species he was unable to access commercially. He also husbanded quantities of hard-to-purchase plants that were being destroyed on neighbouring properties.

Surrounded by the grandeur of the Winterhoek mountain range and its unique vegetation, this garden in the Tulbagh valley brings together different vegetation types to establish harmony and symbiosis between the wilderness and the new residence.

Patrick's work with Van Biljon has made it possible for threatened species, like those of *Babiana*, for instance, that generally grow between rocks for protection against feasting porcupines, to spread and thrive in the landscape. Other species, like Chincherinchee or Tjienks (*Ornithogalum thyrsoides*), also grow here, while some inedible *Moraea* and *Homeria* species have been able to find display areas out of their typical habitats.

The owner's collection of cycads has been given an open space but, so as not to disturb the ambience of the rest of the gardens, a 'cycad sculpture park' was created that is separate from the main garden. It has its own 'room', enclosed by a hedge of Breede River Yellowwood (*Podocarpus elongatus*), where each cycad specimen is given maximum space, allowing the visitor to appreciate the various forms and see them as artworks in their own right. Alongside the cycad area, an extensive food garden has been planted in raised beds to feed the owner's family and the staff who work on the property.

Located on the slopes of the Winterhoek Mountains, the wild renosterveld in the hills surrounding the formal garden provides an ever-changing backdrop for new plantings to be appreciated as the seasons pass. This type of planting allows for a freedom and playfulness that is evident in Patrick's later works. Painterly in their layering, the beds are packed full of Fauve-style palettes and dense textures that clash and collide. That the various species coexist, and thrive together, only makes their abundant flowering more spectacular to witness.

In contrast to the central lawn and neoclassical architecture of the residence, the expressive use of planting also connects the space into the atmosphere of the wilder environment beyond, blurring the lines between the formal and the wilderness.

RIGHT Bright bursts of yellow from Coulter Bush (*Hymenolepis crithmifolia*) shine between pale mounds of helichrysums and Renosterbos (*Dicerothamnus rhinocerotis*) within the beds, framing the central lawn of the main residence and the 'cycad sculpture park', which is separated from the rest of the landscape by a tall hedge.

FOLLOWING SPREAD An aerial view over the private gardens of Daraheen Farm reveal sculptural elements, such as the owner's cycad collection, as well as the vegetable garden, which feeds both family and staff.

The beauty of these renosterveld and fynbos plants is a rare sight in a village where surprisingly few gardens have embraced their use. But, with the help of specialist nurserymen like Van Biljon, greater varieties and quantities of renosterveld and fynbos species are being cultivated for domestic use in the area. Renosterveld is among the most threatened vegetation types in South Africa, and so the use of locally indigenous and endangered plants in this setting creates a viable alternative to the general preference for exotic plants. Van Biljon is passionate about encouraging their use in private landscapes, and regularly takes visitors to the site to appreciate their importance in domestic conservation.

The restoration of the riverine forest has set a benchmark for the neighbouring farms to follow. Species that have been introduced to the river banks, such as Wild Almond (*Brabejum stellatifolium*), are beginning to naturalise, creating healthy stands once more. Slowly but surely, the neighbouring landowners are changing their attitude towards river conservation. At first, as Van Biljon explains, the local farmers did not understand why a private owner would invest so heavily in the restoration of the river. Now, he says, residents are realising that the overall functionality of the restored ecosystem, and the improved quality of the river water, has added a great deal of value to the land. Restored habitats, he argues, should be regarded as an asset, rather than merely decorative, or existing solely for draining the fields. The work done to date has increased the diversity of the birdlife, greatly reduced soil erosion, and reduced the return of invasive plants. It has created a space in which both the owner and the wildlife can settle in peace. Other unique methods of restoration, such as using Nguni cattle to mimic natural grazing patterns, has also considerably improved the restoration process.

This pioneering restoration project has been recognised as exemplary by conservation bodies, who have commended the approach to extend the work beyond the boundaries of the formally conserved areas. Van Biljon, Patrick and the owner are now working with local government departments to increase the scope of the riparian restoration, with the garden being used as an example of how this can be done effectively, and beautifully.

Daraheen Farm 61

ABOVE AND OPPOSITE The sculptural qualities of the cycad collection are emphasised by natural stones, and paths of gravel that wind between meadows of fynbos and renosterveld.

ABOVE AND OPPOSITE The pale grey leaves of Renosterbos (*Dicerothamnus rhinocerotis*) set the base in the flower beds between a diverse selection of helichrysums and romantic tufts of flowering pink Ruby Grass (*Melinis repens*), also known as Natal Red Top.

"Around the house, I wanted it to be renosterveld, but more like typical garden plants that flower a lot and are conventionally pretty, unlike the renosterveld pioneer species from the area that we typically think of, and which will take over eventually, like the locally indigenous grasses, for instance."

OPPOSITE AND ABOVE The rusty plumes and teal-green leaves of the Giant Honey Flower (*Melianthus major*), which has been planted alongside the pool and elsewhere throughout the garden, layer the landscaping with height, colour and texture.

> "I think the point is always to try and create an appropriate sense of place, so your garden is unique from others around the world. Our plants are special, and the plants from that place are special. That's why you should plant a garden like this."

4
WATERFALL ESTATE
Midrand, Johannesburg
Highveld • Prairie • Suburban

OPPOSITE AND ABOVE In keeping with the contemporary farmhouse architecture of the residence, the garden design makes use of a minimalist planting palette that is dominated largely by ornamental African Weeping Lovegrass (*Eragrostis curvula*).

Patrick explores the juxtapositions between Johannesburg's Highveld grasslands and the city's mine dump 'mountains', as he describes them, in an 8,000-square-metre garden situated in a private residential estate in Midrand. An area halfway between Johannesburg and Tshwane, Midrand forms part of a vulnerable Highveld Grassland biome that has, over two decades, become a dense residential node. Today, little remains of this rolling topography, and thus in 2016, Patrick began working to restore a pocket of the original landscape around the home, where it could be protected and provide sanctuary to displaced insects and birds. Featuring primarily a single species of grass, the common African Weeping Lovegrass (*Eragrostis curvula*), the garden is a nostalgic echo of what once was, and a hopeful vision of a more sustainable future for the area.

IN SETTING OUT THE INITIAL DESIGN, Patrick worked with the homeowner's architectural brief to create a proposal that responds to the contemporary farmhouse-style plan, but which also looks further to the surrounding context, where the ghosts of Johannesburg's mine dumps have served as inspiration for the design. Using the 45-degree slopes so emblematic of the dumps, Patrick planted blocks of prairie-style fields in terraces along the contours of the site, and filled them with eragrostis. Between the terraces, mown golf course-quality grass paths echo the estate's golf course, as well as the personal history of the homeowner, who has South African golfing history in her blood.

The design, a quintessential example of Patrick's pioneering veld-style gardens, combines a bold contemporary language with romantic planting that is attuned to the surrounding landscape. Requiring little maintenance other than the upkeep of the paths, and a minimal amount of water to sustain, the garden offers a climate-friendly and relatively affordable alternative to the city's more traditional domestic gardens. The reintroduction of keystone species such as *Eragrostis curvula* has, since planting, been extended accross the estate, creating a self-sustaining and self-regulatory stable ecosystem that restores elements of the area's unique biodiversity.

OPPOSITE The sloped site has been terraced for a gentle walk, framed by a series of raised beds whose side shaping is designed to emulate the form of the mine dumps so synonymous with Johannesburg's history.

ABOVE The Highveld feeling is brought into focus with a sculptural Paperbark Thorn (*Vachellia sieberiana* var. *woodii*).

PREVIOUS SPREAD When viewed from above, the garden's patchwork textures and minimalist planting palette create a striking complement to the simplicity of the architecture.

OPPOSITE AND ABOVE The straight lines of the lawned pathways provide a formal complement to the grassland-inspired beds, which have been steel-edged to further emphasise the boundary where lawn and veld grass meet.

Waterfall Estate

5
CAPE CLASSIC
Bishopscourt, Cape Town

Formal • Forest • Sunset

Patrick broke ground on a sunset garden, designed to maximise one of Cape Town's most extraordinary late-afternoon views, in 2015, exploring ways to incorporate the view into the landscaping, and expanding the extent of the garden into its forested surrounds. Set across a 7,000-square-metre slope atop a hill in the picturesque suburb of Bishopscourt, the design looks to the Japanese philosophy of Shakkei, or 'borrowed scenery'. It unfolds at carefully positioned pause points, where the ancient forests of Table Mountain and the Constantia green belt appear framed between trees, or reflected in pools of water.

THE PLANTING OF THE GARDEN, which forms part of a family's private estate, connects the site with the Cape Dutch-style architecture of the main residence. The plan reinterprets European classical garden design, but prioritises local plants that echo the forms of familiar northern hemisphere species. Patrick describes the style as Cape Classic – where dense tree plantings connect with wide lawns laid out in formal geometries, framed by flower beds dotted with topiary shrubs and rustic gravel paths that culminate in intimate garden 'rooms'.

During construction, the site's west-facing orientation and wind-free conditions provided a unique opportunity to plant more tree species that could establish themselves in the moist soil, creating miniature forests throughout the garden. This reforesting of the site, as well as sinking the level of parts of the garden, like the swimming pool, below the primary ground level, has created areas of comfortable shade. Tall plantings with hidden areas behind them provide visual screening from the road facing the property, creating a natural privacy shield and a barrier for the rest of the plants from the elements.

The design of the garden unfolded for Patrick and the team, led by Iwan Roux of Rekopane Landscapes, as a largely organic process where the majority of the design decisions were made on site as the project grew. Important and often abstract considerations, like selecting areas with the best views, involve for Patrick a level of intuition that can only be included and planned for in the final planting of the landscape as they begin to reveal themselves. Often, this is only once excavation is under way, requiring a client to commit to the philosophy of their landscape as much as they do to Patrick's vision. This ever-evolving relationship between landscaper, client and garden grows as the project develops, creating a collaboration that

OPPOSITE A reflection pool mirrors the extraordinary view out over Table Mountain. As its surface image changes throughout the day, the broader landscape is brought back into the garden itself.

also extends to the craftsmen working on the project, allowing their niche skills to contribute to the complete environment as it manifests. Patrick has worked in this on-site mode of design since his earliest projects, among them Sun City, abandoning the creation of drawn plans to allow the project to respond to the site itself.

Alongside the new plantings, the team has made great efforts to undertake a partial restoration of the surrounding forest of locally indigenous Yellowwood Trees (*Podocarpus* spp.) and other Western Cape Afromontane species. Today this unique vegetation is flourishing again, full of Wild Peach (*Kiggelaria africana*), Spoonwood (*Cassine peragua*) and other historical species that had been compromised by nearby development and the introduction of invasive species by the Cape's early colonial foresters.

The restoration of indigenous species throughout the Table Mountain National Park has been a project of national importance for decades, and it is thanks to a commitment to responsible gardening practices by neighbouring properties, such as the restoration work undertaken by the owners of this garden, that biodiversity is rapidly expanding along the east-facing slopes of the mountain, and throughout the southern portion of the Cape Peninsula.

> "The Japanese love the moon, and moonlight on their plants, which is beautiful. But in this garden, it is really the sunset that I wanted to make the focus. It's rare to have a place where you can watch the unpredictable drama of the Cape's weather, which seems to change every fifteen minutes. One moment it's wild against the landscape, and then the next, it is harmonising with it."

ABOVE The extraordinary view from the garden became central to the design, with a reflection pond settled into the lawn bringing the view into the landscaping itself.

FOLLOWING SPREAD The property benefits from little wind and high rainfall, allowing the design to focus on reforesting the garden, helping to reconnect it with the remnants of Afromontane forest it neighbours.

ABOVE AND OPPOSITE Pine trees, introduced in colonial times, frame an extraordinary view towards the mountains. The view became the central focus of the design, incorporating opportunities to appreciate it through elements like a shallow reflection pond and pause areas along a route that winds around the property.

ABOVE AND OPPOSITE Areas of the garden have been terraced, or sunk below the level of the residence, and enclosed by natural stone walls, creating intimate spaces from where one can appreciate the views.

"A building has a roof and four walls. But you can't draw what's underneath the ground, or elements like a view, for instance. You can make a diagram as a concept, but not exact working drawings, where every little stone is put in place. For years, people have always asked me, 'Why don't you draw a plan?', but unless you stand on the site, and you react to the site when you're standing there, it's too complicated to draw in detail. There's so much you can't pick up. It's not on a plan, it's not on a drawing, and every day it's different."

Natural stone walls surrounding the sunken swimming pool have been plugged with herbs and flowering creepers to soften the hard edges.

6
MORULENG CULTURAL PRECINCT
Moruleng, North West Province

Medicinal • Arid • Educational

In the park grounds of the pioneering Moruleng Cultural Precinct in North West Province, Patrick has partnered with the Bakgatla-ba-Kgafela community, local government and an award-winning architectural practice to create a 'desert museum' that explores the influence, heritage and legacy of southern African traditional medicine.

SINCE THE LAUNCH OF THE PROJECT IN 2015, the Moruleng community have been active participants in the evolution of the garden. They continue to contribute their own plants to the collection, revealing more stories of the area's immense botanical, geological and social history, and expanding on the place these precious plants hold in their lives. Anchored by arid species that have been sparsely planted across a dramatic hectare of hewn rock fields, the garden appears as a museum in itself, and continues the uncomplicated approach to narrative that is used within the precinct's exhibitions.

OPPOSITE AND ABOVE Tall Bushveld Candelabra Trees (*Euphorbia cooperi*) punctuate the rock and gravel of the Moruleng Cultural Precinct's public park, where a medicinal garden, planted between historical structures and cultural artefacts, tells the story of the Tswana community who call the area home.

Project architect Nabeel Essa, founder of architectural practice Office 24/7, who led the design of the precinct and site, describes the landscape as a 'tapestry and exposed palimpsest' that layers the site's narratives together. Their shared vision for the landscaping begins in the creation of a paved route that moves between recent additions, upgrades to heritage structures, and informational infrastructure, with rock seating enclosures punctuating the journey.

Alongside the path, curved parterres have been filled with mining waste rock salvaged from nearby sites between which hardy succulents such as *Dracaena hyacinthoides* and *D. aethiopica* send their spear-like leaves skyward, drying into dramatic brown spikes in winter. Eschewing the use of other ground covers, the stark and sculptural rock base is broken by the towering candelabra-like branches of *Euphorbia cooperi* and *E. ingens* and the gnarled trunks of drought-friendly trees that are associated with functional medicine within the community, such as Marula (*Sclerocarya birrea*), Kanniedood (*Commiphora* spp.), several local fig (*Ficus*) species and *Vachellia karroo*.

Some fascinating, although at times dangerously toxic, plants such as African Climbing Onion (*Bowiea volubilis*) are dotted around the landscape, continuing the development of in situ traditional medicine conversations. Now facing severe threat in the wild due to over-utilisation, but gathered from the muthi (traditional medicine) markets to be propagated by Patrick, the bowiea and other threatened species – such as Bush Saffron (*Cassine transvaalensis*), which is imperilled by herbalists who harvest its bark for its emetic properties – are invaluable additions to the garden. These species are also protected by the community who use the garden.

'I remember explaining the Moruleng Cultural Precinct project to Patrick and observed as his mind immediately animated the brief in terms of specific plants and natural materials,' Essa says. 'It's as if he reads the world through the lenses of plants and landscape. The project used locally sourced planting and rocks and Patrick's process is very hands-on. When he is on site positioning plants, you realise the genuine passion he has for what he does. The landscaping is really dramatic and still contextual, 'wild' but still habitable, and the contrast with the heritage buildings emphasises the palimpsest of the site and the museum narrative.'

ABOVE Elephant's Toothpick (*Dracaena pearsonii*) is a popular medicinal plant.

OPPOSITE Bushveld Candelabra (*Euphorbia cooperi*) and Mother-in-law's Tongue (*Dracaena hyacinthoides*) grow between the rocks, overlooked by a reconstructed Tswana hut.

FOLLOWING SPREAD Repetition of mass planting of single species throughout the project allows the landscape to disappear in areas, and the unique architectural elements to become the focus of the project.

"The plants have been positioned quite sparsely to create the sense of the garden being a museum in itself. Two cultures meet here, and we have tried to suggest this by using stone-laying techniques that reference the original stone village that was destroyed by Mzilikazi's Ndebele in the 1820s and 1830s. We didn't plant ground covers because of their high maintenance and need for water, so whatever is planted has to look after itself."

ABOVE AND OPPOSITE The site's layering of historical narratives unfolds as you move through the project, where Western and Tswana traditional architecture and landscaping live alongside one another.

"In a way, the Moruleng garden is an example of what anyone could do in their own garden if you wanted to use plants like these for your medicines, but also how it can take place on a larger scale in parks and other public spaces."

Moruleng Cultural Precinct

LEFT Bushveld Asparagus (*Asparagus laricinus*).

OPPOSITE River Lily (*Crinum macowanii*) and Bushveld Candelabra or Norsdoring (*Euphorbia cooperi*).

"Muthi plants are extremely important ecologically. But at the moment there is little control of the muthi trade and it has damaged the natural ecology of many areas. The muthi trade continues to grow, and despite some attempts at cultivation, the demand is unceasing. It means that the veld is now being exploited unsustainably. The solution is to establish more nurseries around the country in which to grow these plants and even reintroduce them to their native habitats so that we take pressure off the wild species."

7
BIRDSVIEW ESTATE
Inanda, Johannesburg

Theatrical • Parkland • Art

Suburban birdlife finds sanctuary behind the nondescript walls of Birdsview Estate, a 1.2-hectare park and sculpture garden in the heart of the Sandton central business district, designed by Patrick in two phases – first in the early 2000s and then again in 2009. Using sculptural land formations, narrow concrete paths and striking lighting that brings the project to life as night falls, the dramatic landscape is a tribute to the owner's background in the theatrical arts, and highlights his commitment to restorative gardening.

LEFT Sculptural works by Deborah Bell, Norman Catherine and others wind their way up a rock valley excavated to make way for the project's next life as a housing development.

ABOVE AND RIGHT Winter brings the warm reds of Cottonwool Grass (*Imperata cylindrica*) as well as the pale greys and yellows of drying indigenous grasses to this residential garden, creating an attractive and neutral base for the display of large-scale contemporary South African sculpture.

"Johannesburg aspires to glamour and gold. The city started with the most glitzy mineral in the world, and has always attracted theatrical characters with rather impressive personalities. The owner of the garden, a businessman with theatrical training, is a rather charismatic personality, so we wanted to create a sense of the dramatic, with some Hollywood-style glamour added in as well."

THE PROJECT BEGAN WITH THE CREATION of a 40-metre-long rock gully situated beneath the canopy of towering jacaranda trees, around which the owner's collection of cycads could best be appreciated, and protected within beds of Aechmea 'Burgundy' bromeliads that line the paths and surround the cycads.

Patrick's later work on the rest of the garden started with a catchment pond that extends the landscape into a picturesque-style parkland of rolling lawns, lakes and pools set amidst tall willows and islands of grassland-type plantings. Throughout the garden, Patrick has positioned the more monumental works from the owner's collection of contemporary southern African sculpture, forming landmarks that appear along a walking route.

During the creation of the garden, certain portions of the estate were being subdivided for a new housing development to be erected over portions of the property. In anticipation of this next phase of the garden's life, Patrick dynamited the rock around where the housing would be constructed, and then left the boulders exposed as sculptures of their own. In the rainy season, the ravines of the craggy rock faces in the excavation fill with water, reflecting the trees overhead and creating habitats for birds as the water flows into a dam at the bottom of the slope. Exotic species of ducks that were introduced by the owner have made a home for themselves on the ponds and among this rock waterway.

While plans for future residential development have been put on hold at Birdsview, this sanctuary for birds remains. Patrick continues his work on the property, and on others being developed concurrently with the client across southern Africa.

ABOVE Narrow concrete paths wind between the lawns, allowing visitors to view the artworks from various aspects.

OPPOSITE The ponds attract waterbirds throughout the year, and provide unique areas to display artworks, like this sculpture by Deborah Bell.

ABOVE AND OPPOSITE *Aechmea* 'Burgundy' bromeliads line the extraordinary cycad gulley, where artworks that emulate the site's natural rock, such as the sculpture pictured here, by artist Angus Taylor, speak to the landscaping itself.

"Every person is different, and each garden should also be different. I am learning more and more that it is important to give owners what they want for their garden, because if they don't absolutely love it, understand the vision behind it, and how it works in their personal environment, then I have seen repeatedly that it never works, and never will. So one has to design for the clients, and allow them to inform what you do."

8
LOST CITY
Pilanesberg,
North West Province

Tropical • Hospitality • Fantasy

The Sun City complex, situated about 50 kilometres north of Rustenburg in North West Province, spans over 30,000 hectares at the edge of an extinct volcano. The landscaping – one of Patrick's first professional commissions – began in 1979, starting with the original Sun City Hotel and Casino landscape, and the planting of the Gary Player Golf Course and Country Club. Over the course of a decade, the project would expand to include the Cabanas and Cascades Hotels, both designed as mini-resorts; a vast water network of artificial lagoons, lakes, streams, waterfalls and ponds; a timeshare-based Vacation Club; and an environmentally pioneering crocodile sanctuary and tourism park.

IN 1992, SUN CITY'S SIGNATURE OFFERINGS – the Palace of the Lost City, the Lost City Gardens, Lost City Golf Course and the Valley of the Waves water park and beach – opened to the public. For scale, design, botanical diversity and time-to-completion, the landscaping of Sun City remains one of South Africa's most wildly ambitious projects, and one that Patrick continues to work on to this day.

The Lost City Gardens saw some 440 gardeners planting over 1.6 million plants across 25 hectares, including 61,000 lilies, 10,000 exotic orchids, 300 species of palm and 6,000 established trees, all in just over two years. In total, the team working on the project at the time recorded 3,200 different species of plants, shrubs and trees sourced from 14 countries, many of which were grown from seed by expert horticulturalists in purpose-built dry and wet nurseries around the country, and within the Sun City complex itself.

Today the garden incorporates rivers, streams, waterfalls and lakes, and paths overgrown with ferns and cycads. Shade-loving undergrowth thrives beneath a towering canopy of trees, dominated by an extraordinary collection of *Ficus* species (including mature specimens transplanted from elsewhere), as well as Jacaranda (*Jacaranda mimosifolia*), Fluted Milkwood (*Chrysophyllum viridifolium*) and Red Beech (*Protorhus longifolia*).

From above, the extent of the Lost City Gardens becomes clear, with natural dry bush surrounding the planted tropical garden adjacent to the hotel.

Guests and patrons are surrounded by the landscaping, which immerses them in the fantasy of a lost city hidden within a forest.

Designed to be the jewel in the crown of Sun City, the Lost City Gardens began with the hotelier and founder of Sun International, Sol Kerzner (1935–2020). His vision was of a 'jungle' landscape within which the Lost City's mythology could come to life – one based on a fictional story of an ancient African city 'discovered' between the undergrowth. Patrick approached Kerzner's idea of a 'jungle' as a collection of 'micro-forests', as he describes them. Hundreds of palms, as well as a collection of established baobabs (*Adansonia digitata*), were transported in batches. Thousands of epiphytic orchids were displayed on the rough-barked limbs of jacarandas, which served as hosts thanks to the use of special propagation techniques. Most of the orchids have, however, been neglected in later years.

Numerous thorn trees were planted in clusters, along with other tree species radiating out from rich tropical plants at the centre of the design. The 'Silver Forest' focused largely on light-grey-leaved specimens, including cycads such as the spiny *Encephalartos horridus* and Karoo Cycad (*Encephalartos lehmannii*), and clumps of darker grey *Festuca ovina* 'Glauca' grasses. The surviving Silver Clusterleaf or Silver Terminalia (*Terminalia sericea*) glisten in the sunlight, edging onto the outer rim of the dry forest, overlooked by the turrets of the Palace Hotel in the background.

A large thicket of Sesame-bush (*Sesamothamnus lugardii*) grows richly, the fascinating bulbous trees planted closely together. They were acquired from infrastructural development nearby, after being bulldozed out of the ground for the building of a road, and planted on sloping, well-drained, sandy ground, duplicating their natural habitat. Seventy-five of the Lost City tree species are indigenous to southern Africa.

Visitors to the Lost City can climb a tower to view the property from above, where Patrick's vision for the garden's 22 micro-forests are visible. The line between the indigenous bushveld surrounding the resort is also clear from above, gradually fading into the drier forests that become more tropical towards the inner ring of the garden.

Escaping into the levels of fantasy required to create the forest illusion meant consultation with similar hospitality developments across the globe, such as the Disney Parks and Experiences group, that have created resorts nearing this scale internationally. Wildlife experts were also included in the planning of the jungle landscapes to make the fantasy more tangible, resulting in the introduction of exotic birds, such as tropical parrots, into the grounds. Indigenous wildlife was also drawn to settle within the forest from the neighbouring Pilanesberg National Park. Over 190 avian species have been sighted in the forest since its inception, including South Africa's national bird, the Blue Crane, and returning African Ibis.

Kerzner, in an interview with the author in 2020, described his first experience of the site with Patrick before developing the landscape. 'You know, if you saw what we saw when we flew over the first time with a helicopter… well, I must've been mad. It's just incredible what we achieved,' he said in his familiar South African-American accent. He also explained, smiling, how he came to give Patrick the Lost City commission at such a young age: 'I spoke to the trees, and they recommended him.'

Patrick describes his years of working with Sol and Sun International as something akin to film production, and sees the gardens as film sets. Yet, far from a pastiche, today the gardens are seeding themselves, and becoming gradually wilder, with greater numbers of birds, insects and other small animals settling within the landscape. Many of the original exotic species have sadly been lost, as maintenance on the site has become gradually more difficult, but work continues on the gardens, refining the experience and reintroducing greater numbers of indigenous species to the Lost City gardens that are more waterwise and maintenance friendly.

ABOVE Artificial waterfalls and rivers flowing throughout the landscaping, bring life, sound and humidity into the forest areas.

OPPOSITE A monumental Common Wild Fig (*Ficus thonningii*) grows between rocks in a courtyard.

In contrast to the tropical-inspired Sun City Golf Course, the Lost City course moves towards a semi-desert design theme with extensive landscaping in the out-of-play areas. The bunkers are washes of brownish sand, called waste bunkers in certain countries. In the sand are various indigenous *Euphorbia* species, such as Bushveld Candelabra (*Euphorbia cooperi*) with its strange thorny stems, along with densely tufted grasses. The reed-like Crane Flower (*Strelitzia juncea*) has been planted in the rough, appearing like a desert bulrush. A series of elevated stone-clad tees add to the semi-desert ambience, with a large splash of lilac-flowered Wild Garlic (*Tulbaghia violacea*) to the side of the fairways. Zimbabwean stonemasons were employed to realise the complex dry-packing of the natural rock around the tees. Groupings of Mountain Aloe (*Aloe marlothii*) frame the greens on the course, with succulent *Pachypodium* species, some from Madagascar, in the rough.

A number of the scarlet-flowered *Erythrina* species, including Plough-breaker or Ploegbreker (*E. zeyheri*), with its massive underground rootstock, Dwarf Coral Tree (*E. humeana*), and Common Coral Tree (*E. lysistemon*), have been planted adjacent to the clubhouse. Areas of landscaping on the golf course extend the overall concept of the Lost City landscape.

Together with owners and operators Sun International, Patrick and the founding team aim to see the garden recognised as a renowned collection of plants, both for its extraordinary scope and to ensure the protection of its botanical diversity for future generations. New plans are under way to connect all of the gardens into a singular landscape that can be explored along one route, while significant investment has been put in place to create an updated landscape maintenance programme that prioritises the preservation of rare specimens, while also making space for the introduction of new varieties.

"The brief was to create a 'tropical jungle', but I wanted the Lost City gardens to be more than just jungle. So I divided it into different kinds of forests… dry forests, orchid forests, tropical forests. I made a diagram, I still drew plans at the time, and once I had decided what I wanted, we started growing and sourcing plants from all over Africa. Two years later, I actually went and planted everything on site myself, pointing out where the thousands of plants would go by throwing coloured sticks on the ground, a technique I still use on large projects today. We must have thrown about 200,000 different coloured sticks around the property. They were colour-coded in terms of what plant would be planted where, to create the sense of randomisation that happens in nature."

LEFT The gardens of the Lost City hold one of the largest collections of *Ficus* anywhere on Earth, all of which were planted by Patrick and his team, including the biblical Sycamore Fig (*Ficus sycomorus*).

Lost City 115

"I planted tropical plants in the middle, then gradually planted drier veld plants towards the edges, because integration and context is central to a project like this, even when fantasy is the brief. I wanted the garden to eventually become part of the bushveld that surrounds it, because that's how it will survive, and become its own natural forest."

LEFT Unusual forms, like the white form of the South American Kapok Tree (*Ceiba insignis*), with its prickle-covered trunk, have been planted en masse across the lawns.

ABOVE The extent of the project's ambitious landscaping can be viewed from observation towers above the hotel.

Lost City 117

PREVIOUS SPREAD Several fully grown African Baobab (*Adansonia digitata*) were transplanted into the garden after nearly being felled at a nearby development. Rare *Alluaudia procera*, from Madagascar, sends its spiky tendrils skyward.

ABOVE The crowns of hundreds of Mexican Fan Palm (*Washingtonia filifera* var. *robusta*) rise above the forest canopy.

OPPOSITE Palm fronds emerge around every corner, including on the Palace of the Lost City's architectural mouldings.

9
NORTH ISLAND
Seychelles, East Africa
Private resort • Tropical • Restorative

After almost a century of degradation through economic overuse, North Island, a privately owned island in the Indian Ocean's Seychelles archipelago, has been turned into a multi award-winning luxury resort that is redefining the possibilities of ecotourism. Rehabilitation of the 200-hectare island, located some 40 kilometres from the eastern coast of Mahé, the main island of the Seychelles, began in 2002, led by Patrick and Wilton Sikhosana (who is today based at Spier Estate). Following their two-decade-long effort, the property is seeing highly threatened indigenous flora and wildlife returning to the forests and white beaches, ushering in a wave of conservation practices spearheaded by the island's new environmental custodians.

LEFT Few islands in the Seychelles archipelago offer tourists and visitors the opportunity to experience a restored landscape, but North Island's unique approach to ecotourism has created a rare insight into how the landscape may have appeared before being damaged by agricultural exploitation.

ABOVE Located within the 'inner islands' of the Seychelles archipelago, North Island is a privately owned luxury resort and nature conservancy that is redefining the way hospitality projects approach ecotourism.

OPPOSITE In working towards a sustainable restoration programme that references the island's tradition of coconut farming, Patrick identified a portion of the original plantation that would maintain the historical narrative, but wouldn't pose a threat to the survival of the unique indigenous species.

PATRICK HAS BEEN RESPONSIBLE for the rehabilitation of several island landscapes along the African coast, where widespread plantation farming practices, primarily of cocoa and coconuts, led to a severe ecological crisis. The largely uncontrolled 'slash and burn' agricultural approach used in previous centuries had left vast tracts of natural forest in ruin, with invasive species introduced by colonists leaving little of the indigenous flora intact. Patrick's work on restoring the forests of many of these islands has seen him working in São Tomé and Príncipe off the coast of Cameroon, and the complete rehabilitation of Fregate private island in the Seychelles – a project similar in scale to the North Island project.

Patrick began work on North Island in 1997, when he was brought on board by luxury tour operator Wilderness Safaris, which had acquired the island in order to create a resort. The operator's brief placed conservation at the forefront of the development with the aim of creating a 'sense of undisturbed nature' that would offer a glimpse of a pre-agricultural North Island. In keeping with Patrick's approach, the founding team would remove large numbers of invasive species while identifying and retaining established and ecologically unthreatening coconut trees from the original plantation to ensure a connection with the island's past while also giving a nod to the fantasy of island travel.

Patrick's work in similar hospitality settings allowed him to understand the importance of maintaining the fantasy of island travel in the overall design scheme, as tourists expect to find 'postcard-perfect' coconut palms, and long to photograph them.

Patrick and Wilton transplanted trees from undisturbed parts of the island into the developed areas, and worked with neighbouring islands, and nurseries on Mahé, to source further indigenous and endemic specimens, introducing them in planted 'islands' as Patrick describes them.

Groupings of mangrove-loving Fish Poison Tree (*Barringtonia asiatica*), Powder-puff Tree (*B. racemosa*), Tamanu or Tacamahac-tree (*Calophyllum inophyllum*), the local fig (*Ficus rubra*), Zebra Wood or Beach-medlar (*Guettarda speciosa*), flowering Borneo or Pacific Teak (*Intsia bijuga*), and the iconic Coco de Mer palm (*Lodoicea maldivica*), with its distinctive double coconut, one of the largest seeds in the plant kingdom, are now established and thriving across the island. A nursery was created and continues to expand the populations of these beautiful and rare indigenous trees.

RIGHT Establishing 'postcard moments' for photographs is a fundamental part of the design, where pristine white beaches and turquoise water are overhung with palm trees.

OPPOSITE Hard landscaping, like bridges and pathways, has been left to the elements, allowing them to appear as though they have always been there, among indigenous palms.

The North Island team describes the undertaking as their 'Noah's Ark Project', with the dedicated conservation teams continuing to implement Patrick, Wilton and Wilderness Safaris' original restoration programme. An ongoing focus is the eradication of colonies of problematic rodents that pose a threat to the survival of land birds. This immense project has seen the team undertake unique and experimental measures, such as the employment of hunting professionals from all corners of the globe who have worked for over a decade to eradicate these rodents almost completely.

Thanks to the food web of fruit-bearing indigenous flora established by Patrick and Wilton at the start of the project, the island is now seeing the return of rare bird species, like the Seychelles Blue Pigeons, breeding populations of Wedge-tailed Shearwaters and White-tailed Tropicbirds, all in healthy populations. The endangered Seychelles Magpie Robin is also being reintroduced from its original home on Fregate Island. In the 1970s, the Magpie Robin was on the brink of extinction, with a population of only 17 birds recorded on North Island. But hard-working conservation teams at five islands throughout the archipelago have helped the population increase to somewhere over 300 birds.

Shoreline conservation initiatives have also resulted in Hawksbill and Green Turtles beginning to nest on the beaches once more in gradually increasing numbers – a testament to the success of hospitality projects and landscaping initiatives that put conservation at the forefront of their visions.

OPPOSITE In the pool area, lichen- and moss-covered granite rocks, which were excavated during the building process, have been plugged with local ferns and orchids that have since self-seeded and now grow prolifically throughout the built areas.

FOLLOWING SPREAD Three tall *Pandanus balfourii*, known locally as Vakwa Bordmer, and one of four *Pandanus* species that are indigenous to the Seychelles, have been planted beside the pool.

OPPOSITE Various locally indigenous ferns have been planted en masse in the undergrowth and along pathways.

LEFT Fruit trees, like this guava tree, grow wild throughout the landscape.

ABOVE The flowers of the Indonesian Cucumber Tree (*Averrhoa bilimbi*) turn into the bilimbi fruit, an important ingredient in Seychellois culinary culture.

FOLLOWING SPREAD Dirt roads wind around the island, which is surrounded by restored forest that is alive with indigenous animal and plant species.

ABOVE AND OPPOSITE The Seychelles Stilt Palm (*Verschaffeltia splendida*) has been reintroduced and now grows abundantly on North Island. Its slender trunk is supported by prominent stilt roots and the protective spines deter herbivores. This palm has been classified as 'near threatened' in the wild due to widespread habitat loss from human settlement. Thanks to the hard work of the landscaping team, populations of the palms continue to expand and thrive across the island today.

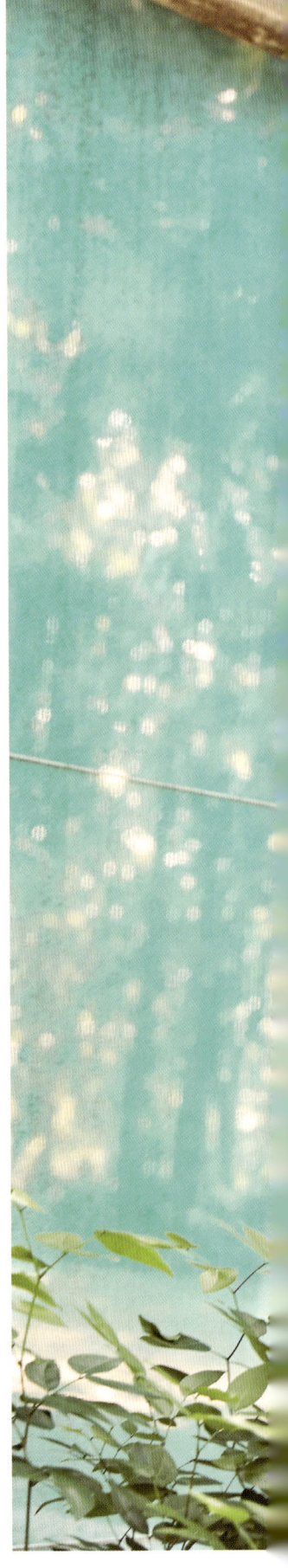

THIS SPREAD Many members of the original team that began the North Island restoration still work and live on the island, like Elliot Mokhobo (opposite) and Elliot Nsele (left), who maintain the nurseries set up by Patrick almost two decades ago. Working with the current custodians of the island, they continue to expand indigenous diversity across the site, creating new nurseries and programmes to remove invasives that threaten the survival of local species.

OPPOSITE The Aldabra Giant Tortoise (*Aldabrachelys gigantea*), one of the largest tortoise species on Earth, is endemic to the Seychelles' Aldabra atoll. Once found on many Indian Ocean islands, they became extinct due to exploitation by sailors from passing ships. Between 80 and 100 tortoises roam North Island free from harm, most of them donations from other islands, and some as old as 150 years of age.

ABOVE Following the eradication of rodents, ground birds such as the Common Moorhen have started settling and breeding across the island again, and it is becoming something of a birder's paradise.

10
NIROX ESTATE
Cradle of Humankind, Gauteng

Land art • Grassland • Serene

In the heart of the Cradle of Humankind fossil hominid area lies Nirox Estate, celebrated for its extraordinary sculpture park, and where several private homes surrounding the park have been landscaped by Patrick. From its former life as a trout farm, the sculpture park has, since opening in 2006, become one of Gauteng's leading tourism destinations. Rolling across 30 hectares of contoured earth mounds and lawn fields, inspired by the forms of the land art movement, the project has also become a pivotal base for nature-based discussions and sculptural interventions that explore our human relationship with nature.

LEFT A series of streams, rivers and ponds connects Nirox Sculpture Park's rolling lawns, forest and riverine vegetation into a singular landscape, bounded on all sides by private properties, hotels and restaurants, all showcasing sculpture and art collected from across the African continent.

Nirox Sculpture Park

The Cradle of Humankind, which spans some 47,000 hectares along the western edge of Gauteng, is less than an hour's drive from Johannesburg's city centre. It was given World Heritage status by UNESCO in 1999 as a Fossil Hominid Site for its large numbers of fossils, including some of the oldest hominin fossils ever discovered, some dating back as far as 3.5 million years. Aside from its outstanding palaeoanthropological wealth, the area is among the province's most picturesque: limestone hills are covered in lush Highveld vegetation, with expanses of grassland disturbed only by dense groupings of indigenous trees and dwellings largely hidden in the landscape.

The Nirox Foundation is a non-profit trust that offers residency opportunities for selected artists, and space for exhibitions, installations and concerts, as well as an outdoor sculpture park and adjacent restaurant, both of which are popular weekend destinations.

For Patrick, the design of the entire Nirox project has always been one that pushes the limits of collaboration, beginning at the outset with the neighbouring residents, and then with the resident artists themselves, who contributed their designs to craft the landscape into its current form. Since then, each of the more than 300 artists who have participated in the Nirox residency programme has added their own works to the landscape, reforming it into an experimental environment that is constantly evolving and redefining itself.

Together, the landscaping and restoration of the waterways, wetlands, dams, rolling grassland and forested areas create a minimal backdrop for some of the African continent's most exciting art installations. The park's loosely defined paths, verdant lawns and glassy water surfaces allow for a level of tranquillity that encourages exploration, or contemplation, with the ever-changing exhibits creating moments of surprise, delight and a renewed connection to the unique landscape in which they reside.

Patrick's design makes the most of the estate's natural spring water and the Blaauwbank Spruit, a river that flows through it, to create a series of aquatic landscapes that connect to each other. Between these reflective expanses, curvilinear beds of grasses, inspired by the Highveld, introduce texture into the landscaping. Within the riverine forests, indigenous White Stinkwood (*Celtis africana*), River Bushwillow (*Combretum erythrophyllum*) and Wild Olive (*Olea europaea* subsp. *cuspidata*) grow in thriving populations around the public areas.

OPPOSITE Picturesque moments are created alongside the river's edge, where installations of contemporary sculpture are exhibited throughout the year, overlooked by exotic trees that are typical of the parkland aesthetic, like romantic Weeping Willows (*Salix* spp.) and Poplars (*Populus* spp.), retained from the site's previous iteration as a trout farm.

LEFT AND ABOVE Creating a minimalist backdrop of green became important in the design of the Nirox Sculpture Park, ensuring that the Foundation's exhibits of sculpture and land art would become the primary focus in the landscape.

FOLLOWING SPREAD The artist residency overlooks a pavilion and several lakes and art installations, the perfect space for contemplation.

Nirox Estate

Nirox Private Landscapes

Part of the Nirox Estate, although not accessible to the public, are homes belonging to the original founders of the estate. In these private gardens, Patrick and the co-owners of the property have worked together over many years to create a neighbourhood connected by shared streams, forests and walkways, but without walls – a community that puts nature and conservation at the forefront of their planning.

Many of the gardens Patrick worked on in the Nirox Estate look toward similar themes as the sculpture park's central proposal but, over time, they have each taken on a distinct landscaping character that speaks to the owners' personalities and individual styles.

In one of these, Patrick undertook an extraordinary three-year process of sensitive excavation, starting in 2015, to reveal the fascinating rock forms hidden beneath dense overgrowth and the sediment of years of agricultural activity. Today, the garden dips and erupts in masses of this ancient rock, marking the landscape with its linear striations that create a graphic pattern throughout the garden. Between and beneath monumental contemporary sculptures are winding streams and wide reflecting ponds in which indigenous aquatic plant species now grow abundantly. Many of the rocks are themselves fossils, ancient stromatolites with layers created by colonies of microscopic cyanobacteria that could photosynthesise and thus create oxygen.

Elsewhere, Patrick exposed the beauty of the river, allowing it to become paramount in the design of a private garden for a patron of the arts and collector of sculpture. Years of neglect had resulted in the river becoming overgrown, with the watercourse blocked in many parts, so Patrick and his team worked to clear sections of the river and reintroduce aquatic plants that would not only enhance the appearance of the riverbed and banks, but also improve the quality of the water itself. Grassland species, introduced in islands to connect the landscape to the veld surrounding it, enliven the islands with flowering species that add interest and variety as the seasons pass.

ABOVE AND OPPOSITE It took many years of excavation to remove the deep layers of sediment that had buried these extraordinary rock formations. Revealing them has created moments of natural sculpture in this private garden, which is separated from the sculpture park by a strip of natural forest.

OPPOSITE AND ABOVE Bridges connect the vast terraces of this private garden on the Nirox Estate, allowing the scale of the gardens to become more intimate and feel connected to the forest beyond each property's private boundaries.

A collection of indigenous grasses and sedges brings texture and movement into the lawn embankments.

THIS SPREAD The restoration of numerous waterways promotes the flow of fresh spring water throughout the estate, from private gardens on the boundary into the public areas of the sculpture park, before continuing on towards the Cradle of Humankind World Heritage Site.

True to its name, Reflection's water gardens are designed to mirror the Cradle of Humankind's breathtaking skyscapes.

ABOVE AND RIGHT At the furthest end of the Nirox Estate, Reflection, one of the private gardens, begins with a breathtaking driveway: a causeway, surrounded on both sides by water, grass and beds of reeds. The median planting, reminiscent of a wagon trail, enhances the sense of timelessness, and a feeling that the landscape has always been this way.

Reflection

At Reflection, one of the longest-running private projects on the Nirox Estate, Patrick has worked in close partnership with Iwan Roux, his longstanding hard landscaping partner, across six hectares to create an aquatic landscape that continues to grow and become evermore imaginative.

The decade-long project broke ground in 2011. At the time, the neglected plot was referred to as 'Crab Farm' because of the profusion of crabs along the banks of the river. It has since become the Roux family's primary residence, with a shed-inspired High Tech-style house, also designed by Patrick (the third dwelling of his career), overlooking their 'water park,' as Roux describes it. The tract of natural land comprises lakes, dams, waterfalls and streams that are interconnected via earth bridges, wide lawns and winding stone paths built largely of rock excavated during the construction of the landscape.

Patrick and Iwan began with the management of tributaries throughout the site, which had become a marshland due to episodes of natural flooding over the years. A 'green pool' was the first project undertaken, after which work began on rerouting the underground springs into the first of Reflection's many lakes, with a wide, curved lawn added to surround the lakes. Excavations for the lakes and dams revealed sculptural outcrops of dolomitic rock. These have since been laid bare above the water surface throughout the landscape, with pools forming between their crevices and furrows filling and emptying as the water levels change with the seasons.

The landscape has also been designed to reconnect to the forest of White Stinkwood (*Celtis africana*) and River Bushwillow (*Combretum erythrophyllum*) that separates the property from its neighbours and the sculpture park.

The architecture of the house integrates the landscape design directly into its planning, starting with the location of the large existing trees around which the concept of the architecture orientates itself. Plotted around these trees, a 38-metre-long glass corridor acts as a central spine, off which the rooms of the house materialise. A stone wall surrounding this 'village of boxes', as Patrick describes it, provides privacy and protects the space from a variety of wildlife that roams the reserve. The volumes of the house have been slung low and the structure is topped with a roof of vegetation, rendering it almost invisible from viewpoints higher up in the landscape. Initially, Patrick looked to farm sheds and greenhouses for a palette of utilitarian finishes that would connect the High Tech architectural detailing (like the expansive glass windows and stainless steel trusses) to the aesthetic of the surrounding countryside.

RIGHT Flat stones form a causeway, allowing cars to pass over a shallow stepped water feature that cascades gently down towards the entrance to the home.

THIS SPREAD Natural materials used in the architecture of the home connect the built areas to the breathtaking surrounds, while the sound of water moving through path-side rills and over gentle waterfalls acts as a 'sound route' that the owners and their guests can follow as they walk through the garden.

Nirox Estate

The minimal planting palette for the garden at Reflection is dominated by local trees, including Stinkwood (*Celtis* spp.) and Bushwillow (*Combretum* spp.), as well as indigenous aquatic lilies and marginal grasses, such as Water Lily (*Nymphaea nouchali* var. *caerulea*), perennial marginal Red or Pink River Flag Lily (*Hesperantha coccinea*), Hedgehog Sedge (*Cyperus congestus*), Floating Hearts (*Nymphoides thunbergiana*) and Wild Mint (*Mentha longifolia*).

The rocks have been placed meticulously on the widespread lawn near the pool, which has been finished with a natural colour that blends into the landscape. A little way away across the lawn are the scarlet-flowered dwarf shrubs known as Ploegbreker or Plough-breaker (*Erythrina zeyheri*). These low-growing plants are endemic to South Africa, with large transparent leaves covered in thorns that protect the foliage and seed pods against herbivores.

In keeping with the name of the property, 'reflection' is a focus of the design throughout the site. Surrounding the pool are small, shining ponds that turn silvery-pink as the sun sets, forming pools of clouds when the sky turns overcast and, at night, collecting thousands of stars in celestial aisles between the lawns and the forests.

The sheer scale of the water that courses throughout the property, a rarity on much of the Highveld, and the dramatic change in vegetation that occurs as you move further from the source of the water, create an ever-changing series of landscape 'events' that unfold as you explore. From the calm of the lawns overlooking the lakes and ponds, to the intrigue of the overgrown fern-filled forests, and beyond to the fine red earth and fossilised rock of the rolling grasslands at the outer reaches of the reserve – each moment invites you to explore deeper.

Alongside this property, two nearby sites are expanding the scope of the project, and will ultimately be connected to Reflection via tunnels and bridges, offering a new dimension to a unique development that is responsible, sustainable, and celebrates the Cradle of Humankind's precious history.

ABOVE AND OPPOSITE Reflection's pool, one of the first elements built on site, looks towards the hills of the Cradle of Humankind.

FOLLOWING SPREAD As you return to the residence, the reflective windows and stone walls first conceal, then reveal, moments in the landscape, adding playfulness and whimsy into the experience of the built areas.

THIS SPREAD The forest is shared between Reflection and its neighbours in a protected nature reserve that includes the sculpture park and homes that border the park, some of which Patrick has also designed. Serpentine embankments separate areas of water and, when viewed from above, make one wonder what ancient secrets may yet arise from beneath this venerable landscape.

ABOVE AND OPPOSITE Alongside a stream are slightly irregular rows of Grassland Tree Fern (*Alsophila dregei*) whose fronds are reflected in the water. The natural stone path leads to a circular firepit and seating area beneath a glade of trees, a perfect spot to sit and contemplate the beauty of this place.

11
iSTORE
Sandton, Johannesburg

Corporate • Lawn • Land art

In the gardens of the flagship Apple iStore in Johannesburg, Patrick looked to the forms of the High Tech architecture movement, the minimalism of the Apple brand, and the linear forms of Johannesburg's highways to create a graphic landscape against the backdrop of the Sandton CBD.

FEATURING LITTLE PLANTING other than lawn grass, slopes were built up and crafted using building waste generated during the construction of the iStore, creating a pair of parallel terraces with grass planes interrupted by rock sculptures and time-smoothed boulders.

Launched in 2009, the project covers 6,000 square metres. It dips down into a dramatic valley, between the terraces, that leads to two catchment ponds at the base of the site, where benches and viewpoints allow visitors to enjoy the vista of the Sandton skyline beyond.

The crash of traffic from the busy road that passes the iStore is almost inaudible from the garden. Set between the skyscrapers, the property is a respite from Johannesburg's relentless urban expansion – and a rare pocket of green, alive with dramatic shadow-play and bold contemporary sculpture amidst the surrounding grey and reflective panels.

PREVIOUS SPREAD The connection between monumentality, engineering and geometry is celebrated in the sculptural landscape design of South Africa's first Apple iStore.

OPPOSITE The garden, featuring a monumental stone sculpture by artist Angus Taylor, overlooks the contemporary corporate architecture of the Sandton CBD and brings a touch of tranquillity and a heady dose of green to one of the area's busiest streets.

ABOVE Terraced grass embankments flow from the balcony of the Apple headquarters in Johannesburg, overlooking a minimalist landscape designed to emulate the graphic simplicity of the Apple devices themselves.

12
THE GREENS

Sandhurst, Johannesburg

Architectural • Minimalist • Structural

In this private family home, Patrick and architect Keith Mason connect a contemporary structure to its suburban surrounds by playing with the language of residential lawns on a large scale. Considering grass lawns to be synonymous with the homesteads of Sandhurst, they constructed a 4,000-square-metre landscape of almost entirely standard lawn grass from which the building appears to erupt.

FOR PATRICK AND KEITH, who have worked together on several projects throughout their careers, the project was considered as a whole, exploring landscape and architecture within a single plan. Patrick responded to Keith's brutalist-inspired architecture by staying true to its minimalist palette. His grass planes are moulded in response to the contours of the architecture: they dip into sunken terraces and rise up constructed ramps. The plain base is occasionally broken by indigenous trees and cycads, but only to soften hard edges and provide shade. Kikuyu grass (*Cenchrus clandestinus*), from East Africa, was selected for its connection to the client, who hails from the same region and who, from the outset of the design process, requested a minimalist feeling from both the architecture and landscape.

THIS SPREAD The focus on standard garden lawn has been carried through into driveways and roof terraces.

"All gardens stand in a landscape, but here, the garden shouldn't take away from the built architecture that Keith has created. So, the simpler the better. Lawn is very much a part of the area's existing language, and we wanted to keep the character of the context in the space."

OPPOSITE AND ABOVE The garden of this private home has been designed to appear as if the architecture has emerged and broken through from below the lawn – a typical element of the area's traditional landscaping language.

'Architecture and landscape have to be totally in tune with each other for something like this to work, and that's what Patrick's designs do. I think that's how he constructs the challenge of his landscapes,' Mason explains.

'The work of his father, modernist architect James Watson, must have rubbed off on Patrick when he was growing up, because he is very much aware of how architects think. He takes an idea that you explain architecturally, and communicates this vision in plants. In this garden we began working with the way the site existed at the outset. There was already a driveway on it, so we wanted to make a home that looks as though it emerges naturally out of the ground from the end of the driveway. It's not a house that is apart from the landscape, but is rather like a stone anchored in the landscape itself, almost as if the garden was there before the house grew up out of it.'

'Often buildings dictate an axis which will extend to form an avenue of trees in many instances, perhaps one that results in an arrival and exit point. But this garden is not like that, it is not an after-event. The experience we wanted to establish is that garden and house are part of each other, and also further integrated with the neighbourhood's trees so that the entire landscape feels connected to itself and beyond.'

OPPOSITE AND ABOVE The design emphasises the sculptural and graphic qualities of the traditional tennis court by sinking the level of the court below the primary ground level, creating sloped sides, and maintaining the use of grass as a singular material throughout.

PREVIOUS SPREAD A sloping upper terrace walkway, planted with both new and established trees, gives the impression of being in a park.

ABOVE AND OPPOSITE Kikuyu grass (*Cenchrus clandestinus*) has been used extensively throughout the site, including on the terrace leading to the tennis court. Although grass courts are not common, it is hard to imagine any other surface here. The court markings, stone steps and trimmed terrace echo the linear lines of the home.

13
STARK STUDIOS
Randburg, Johannesburg

Sculptural • Cinematic • Modular

Five plant pyramids anchor the garden design for a film studio in Randburg, where landscape modules between the facades of the pyramids create a series of 'filmic' frames. These 'cinematic modules' are used as quiet rehearsal areas for off-set actors, backdrops for movies or photo shoots, and outdoor function spaces for the studio offices. Each scene is largely hidden behind the pyramids, creating a maze as one moves between the vertical planting – a riot of vivid colour blocks monoplanted with grass, herbs, succulents and perennials.

THE STARK STUDIO GARDENS, spread over one hectare, represent one of the more playful expressions of Patrick's exploration of fantasy and land art. Completed in 2009, following the creation of other fantastical landscapes like the Lost City and the sculptural forms of the Nirox Sculpture Park, the project brings together two worlds in Patrick's oeuvre, creating an artful island of escape within the studio's suburban surrounds.

At Stark Studios, Patrick has explored axonometry, crafting vast vertical planes of plants intercut with zig-zagging platforms and paths that unexpectedly change levels, concealing the buildings and expanding the landscape's edges. Each 'room' or 'set' that the pyramids create is distinct, resulting in diversity and a 'theatrical ambience', as Patrick describes it, that ties the garden back to its context.

Patrick's goal with the planting palettes was to make the landscape, and each 'scene', instantly photographable – creating an 'Insta-garden'. As production crews will tell you, the scenes consistently are. Aside from large established trees that were retained from the original domestic garden, the majority of the landscape has been newly planted.

The graphic approach to the planting takes inspiration from the postmodernist gardens of Patrick's long-time friend and collaborator Roberto Burle Marx. At Stark Studios, he experiments with colour, contrasting panels of orange-red Campfire (*Crassula capitella* 'Campfire') with banks of lilac Wild Garlic (*Tulbaghia violacea*). Walls of burgundy bromeliads intersect with mondo grass embankments, exploding with texture and pattern. The overall experience can be disorientating at first, and then calming, but at every turn the garden erupts in unanticipated moments of surprise and quiet moments of detail.

The design and accomplishment of the plant pyramids emerged from the construction of the studios themselves, when a mass of accumulated building waste and soil provided an opportunity for reuse in enterprising landforms. (Prior to designing this project, Patrick had worked in a similar way with the owners of the studio in the landscaping of their private home garden, maximising available soil, broken brick and rock to revamp the form of the landscape.)

OPPOSITE The lily pond reflects the changing moods of the sky as clouds pass overhead.

ABOVE Essential stormwater drains have been surrounded by flowering plants, making them appear part of the overall design.

OPPOSITE Grasses and masses of the Satin Flower (*Sisyrinchium striatum*), planted in blocks around the lawn, echo the linear forms of the buildings and landscaping.

An old-fashioned swimming pool, with its high walls now revealed, has been repurposed as an ornamental lily pond, and a stormwater outlet and retention pond have been planted with wetland species, including sedges (*Cyperus* spp.) and bulrushes (*Typha* spp.), arums (*Zantedeschia aethiopica* and *Z. aethiopica* 'Green Goddess') and Highveld Red-hot Poker (*Kniphofia ensifolia*). Water for the pond is captured from the roofs. A zigzag bridge repeats the triangular shapes of the iconic pyramids, and encourages performers to do a slow, silhouetted walk across the wetland.

Shady pathways wind beneath an uneven row of Silver Birch (*Betula pendula* 'Alba') with its light stems and silvery green foliage that turns yellow-gold in autumn. A winding gravel path, lined with River Bushwillows (*Combretum* spp.), forms an avenue of red, purple and orange-yellow in the autumn. Clivias are planted en masse in the undergrowth of the avenues.

More cubist forms and platforms lead down from the main building, creating graphic bands of white steps towards the lawn from the restaurant terrace. A rectangular lawn lined with benches is framed by exotic willow species, one upright and one weeping. The Curly-leaved or Rams-horn Willow is a *Salix babylonica* cultivar with unusual spiral and curly leaves and branches.

Looking back, Patrick says he would have been more minimal with the planting scheme if he got the chance to redo it and would have incorporated more indigenous specimens. Even so, underpinning the drama of the high contrast of his original planting palette is a minimal base from which any sort of landscape could be created in the future. And beyond the planted pyramids is a place where the film industry is able to connect with a small slice of nature in the midst of suburbia, and create its own sanctuary between the bright lights and the make-believe.

Stark Studios 191

LEFT Lawn grass provides a soft and stable surface for impromptu rehearsals, or even for play.

ABOVE The clever use of angles and linear forms is a defining characteristic of the landscaping.

"In a way it's like frames of a movie, or snapshots of scenes. So if you need another sort of landscape you could just stitch them together to create something a bit alien, if you wanted that."

Stark Studios 193

OPPOSITE AND ABOVE Benches provide a place for quiet contemplation, or to gather with colleagues to discuss projects or share a midmorning coffee break. The embankments create a sense of being removed, if only for a moment, from the frenetic activity of the studio.

Stark Studios 195

14
CLIVIA HOUSE
Khyber Rock, Johannesburg
Colour • Perennial • Collector's garden

Set within the surrounds of an architecturally historic house – designed by modernist architect Wilhelm Meyer and altered later by Francois Pienaar, both architects with whom Patrick had worked at the start of his career – this private garden creates space for the owner to showcase rare and treasured plants, and display his extensive collection of clivias, regarded as one of the most unique clivia collections in the country.

THE PROJECT BEGAN IN THE EARLY 2000s with Patrick editing the garden to remove several exotic and 'visually out-of-key' plants, such as existing pines, in order to establish the base for a more indigenous garden. The house was built around giant granite boulders that, Patrick says, created the 'genius of the place'. The initial work looked to the boulders for inspiration: a water feature was crafted of original and manufactured rocks and the existing pool was transformed into a pond for the owner's collection of koi.

RIGHT A large koi pond, just visible behind a tree trunk, converted from a former swimming pool, anchors the entrance to the garden, reflecting the immense collection of *Clivia* specimens, some even growing in crevices in the trees.

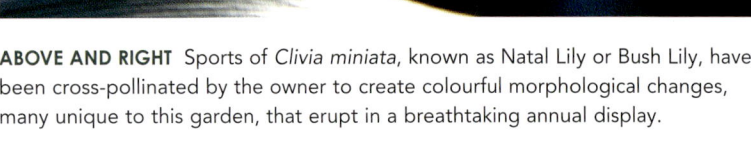

ABOVE AND RIGHT Sports of *Clivia miniata*, known as Natal Lily or Bush Lily, have been cross-pollinated by the owner to create colourful morphological changes, many unique to this garden, that erupt in a breathtaking annual display.

FOLLOWING SPREAD Wild Olive trees (*Olea europaea* subsp. *cuspidata*) create a protective canopy for the shade-loving clivias.

"The client had been growing and propagating clivias for fifteen years before we arrived. We just pulled the collection together artistically, so that when they flowered, you could experience it all together."

On the Highveld, the *Clivia* flowering season is brief, resulting in a garden that is subdued and minimal for most of the year, with the waxy leaves verdant beneath the Wild Olive trees (*Olea europaea* subsp. *cuspidata*). But for two marvellous weeks in spring, the garden comes alive in a bonfire of fiery reds, corals, tangerines and pale yellows – a sight to behold, and a moment in time that is unforgettable.

The owner continues work on the garden, expanding his collection to include species of the poppy genus, as well as other flowering species, to bring moments of colour into the garden when the clivias are out of their flowering season.

ABOVE Stone sculptures, cycads and strelitzias add height and interest to the landscape, particularly when the clivias are not in flower.

OPPOSITE The clean lines of the home's modernist architecture emphasise the uncomplicated landscape design.

15
GARDEN ROMANCE
Craighall, Johannesburg
Romantic • Cottage • Sentimental

Surely one of a designer's most pleasurable tasks must be a creation for a close friend. In the case of this romantic-period inspired landscape, Patrick worked for many years with these friends, and their mutual love for plants has flourished in many gardens in which they have been involved as partners.

IN DESIGNING THIS FAMILY GARDEN in suburban Johannesburg, Patrick created a romantic landscape to reflect the traditional English architecture of the house. The property lies along the banks of a streamlet that feeds the Braamfontein Spruit. The availability of water allowed for the construction of a large garden pond filled with an abundance of water-loving irises at the end of a typical and very beautiful cottage-style garden that has been planted mostly with South African plants.

The 'English cottage garden' as a design genre first became prominent during the Elizabethan era, perhaps as a herb and fruit garden for small properties (hence 'cottage') and the informality of creating gardens in the absence of armies of labourers. It broke away from the conventional by allowing ornamental plants to mix together quite loosely with local wildflowers. This relatively relaxed planting style was given structure through building walls and terraces, often almost covered with flowering climbers. Herbaceous and perennial borders, often self-seeding, also came into fashion, overflowing with colour and texture. And if the cottage garden was sufficiently large, then it was possible to create a series of 'garden rooms' each with a different purpose and a different atmosphere.

ABOVE AND RIGHT Purple Japanese Iris (*Iris ensata*) thrive in water, and have been planted in the clay beds of the home's large pond.

OPPOSITE Yellow flowers fall from an exotic large *Tipuana tipu* tree. Retained in the garden for its age and scale, it grows alongside a variety of indigenous trees, such as Oldwood (*Leucosidea sericea*).

ABOVE The landscape design is inspired by the style of traditional English cottage gardens, which regained popularity during the romantic period of the late 19th century, and which Patrick felt spoke closely to the style of the home's architecture.

OPPOSITE Old-fashioned Arum Lilies (*Zantedeschia aethiopica*), identified by the ivory spathes of their flowers, grow near the water's edge.

Garden Romance 207

In recreating the cottage philosophy in Johannesburg for his friends, Patrick gestured towards Gertrude Jekyll, the great Arts and Crafts garden designer who, fearing the extinction of the cottage garden tradition, revived it in the late 19th century. Using the Jekyll idea and palette, Patrick planted irises of warm colours at the centre of the pond, with cool blue and grey-coloured specimens at the edges. Jekyll had perfected this technique, which she called 'drifting', in the colour-graded flower beds in her own 'hardy flower border' at Munstead Wood, her home in Surrey, where blue and grey flowers merge into yellows, oranges and reds at the centre of the beds.

Surrounding the Munstead-inspired pond, Patrick designed other less formal 'garden rooms'. A visitor arrives at these defined 'rooms' by a winding concrete path that begins at the base of the garden's towering, and very old, pepper tree. The sound of the stream accompanies the walker along the route when entering the first of these rooms, having first to bend beneath the arms of a giant Australian Tree Fern (*Alsophila australis*) to enter into a corner of dense tropical foliage. Continuous mist irrigation maintains the humidity of this tropical area and allows the owners' considerable collection of local ferns and exotic orchids to flourish.

The owners are full of praise for Patrick's sensitive approach. 'Patrick knows us so well that he didn't have to ask what we wanted. He knew we were after something English-styled to suit the architecture, but he also understood that we hankered for something wilder as well. In working with Patrick over many years, one appreciates that he puts the "bones" of the garden in first, a sort of spine. This can take a while to establish and requires patience. But then, slowly, he makes it wilder and wilder. It is almost like a piece of music that gradually becomes more powerful.'

The owners recount an anecdote that characterises Patrick: 'Some years ago, a woman was redoing her Westcliff garden. I had never seen it, but it sounded like a beautiful site. She asked what I thought about Patrick as her designer. I asked her, "Are you patient?" She answered "yes", but the truth is that Patrick's gardens take five years or so before you understand the garden, and what he had in mind for it. So I responded, "If you want to know the difference between Patrick and other garden designers, it's akin to the difference between buying a painting at a jumble sale, or investing in a Monet." He has an amazing gift.'

OPPOSITE Terraced grass steps lead down from the home into the wilder part of the garden.

RIGHT Rose-coloured *Begonia benariensis*.

16
27 BOXES PARK
Melville, Johannesburg
Humble • Community • Butterflies

If anything epitomises the extraordinary variety of creative projects that Patrick has conceived and executed, this Melville community park with its quirky box-like shops is a prime example. Not a gracious home or large corporate enterprise, the park consists of hardy and common 'pavement' plants that uplift the spirits of the residents of Melville, a densely populated and trendy Johannesburg suburb. The 27 Boxes Park – 27 shipping containers selling a variety of wares – is also a sanctuary that augments the public open space of Melville Koppies Nature Reserve located close by. The ridges are famed for 'hill-topping' by butterflies, and 27 Boxes Park provides food plants for butterflies and other small wildlife species.

DESPITE HAVING BECOME A POPULAR tourist and community destination, the park was contentious at its start and almost did not reach fruition. The original open site, named the Faan Smit Park, had become derelict and the municipality sold it to developers as a retail space. However, there was fierce opposition from residents to the construction of a multi-storey shopping mall and there were strong calls for a more community-friendly solution. After intense engagement with local opponents and stakeholders the developer obtained permission to develop the site, but the trade-off was that some of the area become a community park.

OPPOSITE A central concrete path that divides the garden terminates at a spouting water fountain.

RIGHT Intimate seating areas have been surrounded with hardy, drought-resistant Spekboom or Pork Bush (*Portulacaria afra*).

Patrick faced the challenge of crafting a community park within strict budget constraints. To maximise resources, he opted for locally available flora that he was able to salvage or propagate on site. Minimal water usage was also paramount during the park's construction, exacerbated by one of the worst droughts in decades at the time of planting. The succulents collected for the project emerged as the perfect choice for 27 Boxes, thriving with little irrigation.

The garden features a diverse array of 'nondescript' plants – those often overlooked or discarded. Many of these specimens, unsuitable for commercial sale, were gifts from friends or salvaged from neglected gardens. Embracing the resilience of nature, he incorporated pavement-sprung plants, focusing on easy-to-grow varieties such as *Cotyledon orbiculata* and various *Crassula* species.

The centre was constructed using repurposed shipping containers, with the abundant corrugated iron lending the space an industrial feeling. Patrick envisioned the garden harmonising with the architecture, and played with a 'box' motif to achieve a balance between the two.

The landscape plan segments the lot into two rows of eight boxes, bisected by a central concrete pathway. At one terminus stands a fountain, while at the other a communal space invites passers-by and shoppers to explore and reflect. Strategically placed away from the main path are three concrete squares, secluded by towering Spekboom (*Portulacaria afra*) from the Eastern Cape, offering privacy for intimate meetings.

Amidst the verdure, selected boxes have been planted with flora intended to attract birds, bees and butterflies. Tall, majestic trees draw the gaze upwards, notable among them the rapidly growing and water-efficient Wild Pear (*Dombeya rotundifolia*), whose fragrant white blossoms in spring serve as sustenance for some butterfly and moth species. The tree's gorgeous flowers dry gracefully on the branches once the flowering season is over, allowing visitors to appreciate the strikingly pale sprays of desiccated flowers in the cooler months.

RIGHT The 27 Boxes Park has become an important community area for the residents of Melville, in Johannesburg, and a haven for migrating butterflies en route to the neighbouring Melville Koppies.

OPPOSITE Winter brings a wash of vibrant colour to 27 Boxes Park, as well as delicate, dry textures, while in spring there are the papery flowers of the Wild Pear (*Dombeya rotundifolia*).

RIGHT Round-leafed Navel-wort (*Cotyledon orbiculata*), also known as Pig's Ears or Plakkie.

"I was very conscious that the large, open nature reserve of Melville Koppies is not far away, and this means the little park can tap into the botanical and zoological diversity of the region, rather like extending a wildlife corridor. So if a plant is attractive to birds and moths and butterflies, they do come."

ABOVE AND OPPOSITE The leaves of Pondo Cliff Crassula (*Crassula streyi*), also known as Umtamvuna Cliff Crassula, are burgundy on the underside.

RIGHT A variety of flowering plants, including members of the Portulacaceae family and species of *Euphorbia* and *Crassula*, share space in the garden.

17
BOBBEJAANSKLOOF
Plettenberg Bay, Western Cape

Indigenous • Hardy • Coastal

When an extensive overhaul of Bobbejaanskloof Private Nature Reserve was begun in the late 1990s, the landscape was overrun by invasive species. A patchwork of indigenous vegetation now grows wild across the 150-hectare site in the hills above Plettenberg Bay that Patrick describes as a 'bio-mosaic'. Over the years, it has evolved into a complex network of interconnected fragments, where riverine forests meet afrotemperate woodlands and fynbos meadows thrive amidst high-altitude grassland – a style which Bobbejaanskloof's founder (a passionate plantsperson and gardener herself) describes as 'a garden without boundaries'.

THE ORIGINAL SHEEP FARM ON THE SITE had become heavily overgrazed and was overgrown with alien vegetation, so the project began by ringbarking invasive trees and eradicating the wattle entirely. But an avenue of blue gums, which the owner felt added scale and texture to the flat and open topography, was retained.

Hundreds of Outeniqua Yellowwood (*Afrocarpus falcatus*) were simultaneously planted along the boundaries, beginning a planting programme that has continued over two decades, and preceded the architectural developments that would take place once the landscape had settled and established itself.

The broad plan for Bobbejaanskloof included the naturalisation of mass plantings of watsonia, agapanthus and helichrysum in great sweeping drifts that become part of the landscape, while the ongoing eradication of alien species has allowed the locally indigenous vegetation to re-establish itself.

The landscape has been designed to cope without supplementary water. The farm is bisected by a kloof, and is not irrigated, realising the owner's dream to have a garden that would be in tune with the natural cycle of rainfall.

OPPOSITE Fynbos intermingles with grassland species in a style that Patrick refers to as a 'bio-mosaic', flowering throughout most of the year in a patchwork of colours across the landscape.

ABOVE AND OPPOSITE *Helichrysum petiolare*, known as Silver Bush Everlasting, Kooigoed or Imphepho, has re-established itself in immense swathes of silvery foliage, following years of agricultural degradation and overgrazing on the site.

Establishing plants in the area's notoriously hot and windy summer season proved a challenge, but building small runoff dams has been beneficial. Giant Euphorbia (*Euphorbia ingens*) and a collection of aloes, including Cape Bitter Aloe (*Aloe ferox*), add an architectural and sculptural element to the landscape.

The understorey of a section of riverine forest was cleared to make a woodland garden where shade-loving clivias, crinum, White Paintbrush (*Haemanthus albiflos*) and Cape Primrose (*Streptocarpus* spp.) soon became naturalised among the lichen-covered rock, and introduced trees, such as Candlewood (*Pterocelastrus tricuspidatus*), Cape Holly (*Ilex mitis*), Forest Spoonwood (*Cassine peragua*) and Cheesewood (*Pittosporum viridiflorum*) began to take hold.

The delicate epiphytic orchid, *Mystacidium capense*, which grows wild throughout preserved forests in the area, was established on a branch of a pterocelastrus and now thrives throughout the woodland.

A vast grassland area provides a vista of tall specimens, with mown paths forming dramatic walkways through the swaying grass. To provide a link to the nearby Alexandria Forest preserve, large specimens of Coast Coral Tree (*Erythrina caffra*) were transplanted and positioned to break the flatness of the grassland. In summer, their extraordinary crimson flowers provide a counterpoint to the Outeniqua Mountains beyond. To enable the trees to thrive, they were planted in raised mounds, out of reach of a herd of introduced Nguni cattle that graze the grassland in a natural web.

PREVIOUS SPREAD The yellow everlasting flowers of Cape Gold (*Helichrysum splendidum*), also known as Geelsewejaartjie, light up the landscape. The name is derived from the Greek 'helios' meaning sun and 'chrysos' meaning gold.

OPPOSITE Despite being considered invasive, an avenue of blue gums was spared in order to retain a connection between the redeveloped property and its origins as a traditional sheep farm.

ABOVE AND RIGHT Red Watsonia (*Watsonia angusta*).

"The field of grass was for cattle, but when you put one tree in it, a landscape becomes a garden. Trees break the austerity of the landscape."

Bobbejaanskloof

18
STEYN CITY
Midrand, Johannesburg
Rural • Classical • Italianate

Dramatic in scale and notable for the restraint of its planting scheme, the Steyn City development is one of Patrick's longest running commissions, and remains one of his and entrepreneur Douw Steyn's most ambitious undertakings together. Begun in the 1990s, the gargantuan project set out to create a 2,000-hectare indigenous parkland-style residential estate, where newly introduced wetlands, forests and grasslands would provide natural privacy for the residents. The plan was to hide service areas behind walls of foliage, while integrating the lawns and golf courses into the surrounding context. Existing wetlands and protected environmental sites along the river that flows through the estate became priorities, with the focus on restoring damage and enlivening them with new botanical species for greater biodiversity.

RIGHT The golf course fairways are set alongside the river and waterways, while the low-profile clubhouse blends quietly into the vegetation.

FOLLOWING SPREAD Rooftop plantings keep the buildings cool in summer, while also allowing the built environment to merge into the natural landscape when viewed from above.

AT THE TIME OF OFFICIALLY BREAKING ground in 2010 – a decade after Patrick had begun establishing nurseries specifically for the project – much of the site's natural vegetation had been subjected to years of neglect from development occurring on neighbouring properties. Patrick's design set out to restore the broken landscape and, in reimagining the site, required significant new planting to cover an area that is almost four times the size of Kirstenbosch National Botanical Garden in Cape Town, South Africa's largest botanical garden. To create the landscape according to the timelines specified, and within the budget, Steyn City would require over 90 percent of the millions of plants needed for the estate to be grown from seed in purpose-built nurseries on the site – a project that required nurserymen and seed collectors around the country to work with Patrick for more than two decades.

The landscape design is characterised largely by a minimalist planting palette that works to emphasise the scale of the property. Repetition of indigenous species such as Wild Olive (*Olea europaea* subsp. *cuspidata*) and White Stinkwood (*Celtis africana*), along with mass plantings of shrubs, creates a feeling of rhythm as the landscape unfolds.

This project continues Patrick's ongoing work for Douw Steyn, the billionaire founder of a large international insurance and financial group, and instigator of the eponymous Steyn City. Many years ago, Steyn became aware of Patrick's talent and, in the 1980s, commissioned him to design the gardens of his Saxon Hotel in Sandhurst. He later employed Patrick on his safari lodge, as well as other projects over the years. Under Patrick's influence, the Steyn projects have moved away from a more colourful gardening style towards green landscapes that focus on foliage rather than flowering specimens. The client has also invested significantly in the propagation of indigenous plants at other developments, notably Shambala Private Game Reserve in Limpopo and the Saxon Hotel.

OPPOSITE Palazzo Steyn, the owner's private residence, overlooks the estate. During the rainy season, water from its Roman-style aqueducts cascades into the lakes and ponds below.

ABOVE Natural rivers and streams have been dammed to provide year-round water for irrigation, as well as create havens for birds and small mammals that inhabit the estate.

Today, the enormous Steyn City infrastructural development of roads, tunnels, gatehouses, malls, schools, bridges, pumphouses and hundreds of private residences is gradually becoming evermore hidden behind the vegetation of a landscape that, unlike the palm tree-lined estates nearby, celebrates the beauty of Johannesburg's unique flora and fauna, while speaking to the European influence of the estate's architectural identity.

Hundreds of planted Wild Olive (*Olea europaea* subsp. *cuspidata*) augment those growing naturally on the property, some very old. The Wild Olive, also known as African Olive, and other food plants, such as Bushveld Bluebush (*Diospyros lycioides*), grow along the verges and between residences, attracting flocks of fruit-loving birds.

Streams and rivulets form ponds that are surrounded by aquatic and edge plants. Indigenous Cape Willow (*Salix mucronata*) line the waterfalls near Steyn's palatial home, where fast-flowing water is tossed over large boulders before rippling over pebbles at the water's edge. Below the cliffs, waterbirds inhabit the marginal sedges, common reeds and Bulrush (*Typha capensis*), or flit across the pale blue and pink waterlilies. Growing alongside the water are the aptly named Oldwood trees (*Leucosidea sericea*), Ouhout in Afrikaans, whose bark naturally cracks and splits, making them look old even when they are young. Their leathery bark, pinkish underneath, is often festooned with bright yellow lichen and spongy moss.

Masses of fragile Asparagus Fern (*Asparagus virgatus*) have been planted so densely in other areas that they are able to be trained into more formal hedges. So much so that, alongside the Italianate-seeming olive trees, Patrick has been successful in creating an indigenous answer to the client's Tuscany-inspired brief.

ABOVE Mountain Silver-oak (*Brachylaena discolor* var. *rotundata*), also known as Transvaal Silver Tree or Bergvaalbos.

OPPOSITE Indigenous Wild Olive trees (*Olea europaea* subsp. *cuspidata*) are spreading evergreens with glossy grey-green to dark green leaves, greenish-white flowers in spring and summer, and small round fruits that are much loved by birds.

ABOVE Dense plantings of shrubs line walkways throughout the residential portion of the estate, contributing shade in summer, and helping the buildings to merge into the green landscape.

OPPOSITE Maidenhair Fern (*Adiantum capillus-veneris*) hangs from a vertical garden above a water feature in the courtyard of a private home that was landscaped by Patrick.

Steyn City 235

OPPOSITE Stone retaining walls provide structural integrity without compromising the aesthetic. Here, the towering packed stone is reminiscent of Great Zimbabwe and the walls atop the hill at the Mapungubwe Cultural Landscape, creating a visual reminder of stonework that may once have been found over much of southern Africa.

ABOVE The landscaping for the Steyn City Clubhouse and adjacent piazza overlooking the golf course incorporates indigenous trees, as well as rocks that were excavated from the site.

19
ARCADIA
Parktown, Johannesburg

Heritage • Geological • Koppie

PREVIOUS SPREAD Overlooking the Saxonwold forest, and the Magaliesberg in the distance, the Hollard Arcadia campus reconnects several neighbouring properties, many with heritage-graded homes, into a singular, consistent landscape.

OPPOSITE Meeting areas beneath the trees of the koppie garden allow Hollard employees an opportunity to reconnect with nature during their day.

ABOVE Kilometres of serpentine concrete paths, inset with gravel, wind through koppies, forests and the arboretum.

BELOW In the woodland section of the garden, Ribbon Bush (*Hypoestes forskaolii*) creates a wash of white when it flowers in midwinter beneath a canopy of White Stinkwood (*Celtis africana*) and Wild Peach (*Kiggelaria africana*).

At the Arcadia Campus in Johannesburg, two historic gardens have been incorporated into a singlular forward-looking landscape situated across more than 10 hectares of the Parktown Ridge quartzite scarp. Using near-archaeological excavation to reveal the fundamental rock over which the site has been built, archival research into original plans, and a palette of unique high-altitude veld plants paired with long-term, bird-driven seed dispersal, the vision for the project approaches the site's heritage not as a relic, but as an active participant in the process of restoration.

WORK ON THE CURRENT LANDSCAPING STARTED in 2012, with the restoration of the primary garden that surrounds Villa Arcadia, an Italianate Arts and Crafts building dating to 1909. Designed by renowned architect Herbert Baker, the building was commissioned as the home of prominent Johannesburg mining magnate Sir Lionel Phillips and his wife Florence, Lady Phillips, and has since been transformed into an office for the Hollard Insurance Group.

In updating the site, Patrick considered what Baker would have done had he been working on the property today. He began archival research into Baker's original plans for the property, consulted his autobiography, and then looked to the work Florence had undertaken herself to realise the planting, for which she was primarily responsible.

Arcadia 241

"Arcadia has a hundred-year-old history, but our research into the original plans shows that the intention was to be much wilder at the time. New landscaping had layered the site many times since being built, so what we wanted to do was bring back a sort of low-key feeling that needed no irrigation and really prioritises a return to naturalised planting."

OPPOSITE AND LEFT Dry stone walls have been plugged with unusual species such as Blood Lily (*Haemanthus coccineus*), Flat-topped Aeonium (*Aeonium tabulaeforme*), *Sempervivum* and cascading *Crassula* species.

FOLLOWING SPREAD The latest addition to the immense Hollard project includes The Pines, designed by architect JC Watson in 1906, where Patrick has designed a Victorian collector's-style garden, featuring one of the country's largest collections of aloes.

Elements of the 1909 design have been restored, like the stone pathways that reference Baker's other domestic paths in the area, while wide stone steps, which make no reference to Baker's original vision, have been updated into flatter steps, echoing similar designs from his other projects around the globe. Research also revealed the extent of Florence's original plantings, which were identified and preserved to ensure that elements of her founding vision for the gardens remained connected to the building's history.

Florence's now well-established bougainvillea and other Italian-inspired ornamentals have been kept, alongside which Patrick has added specimens that were popular throughout Johannesburg at the time, like the hydrangeas which Florence had also planted prolifically at her other gardens. Many of Baker's favourite indigenous plants, including plumbago and agapanthus, are also used throughout the site.

Baker described the completed gardens at Villa Arcadia in his autobiography as 'A very beautiful garden… that gave a richly coloured foreground to the view over the forest to the distant veld and mountains' – a view that remains among the finest in the city today, especially now that the colourful plantings have been restored.

Importantly for Patrick, the site lacked a distinct landscaping language, as it had been subjected to multiple owners and gardeners during its lifetime. Large portions of the gardens had become neglected and overgrown as a result of being unoccupied for some time prior to its current ownership, and needed to be rehabilitated.

An established woodland with several large indigenous trees and tumbling climbers became the starting point for restoration. Australian Black Wattle (*Acacia mearnsii*) had inhibited the growth of indigenous trees, as it continues to do throughout the Highveld. Once these were removed, Patrick and his landscaping partners introduced colonies of fruit-bearing Highveld trees among the alien, but ecologically unthreatening, hundred-year-old pines, which Patrick felt were synonymous with the area's history and were too old to be cut down.

Parktown Ridge overlooks the suburbs of Saxonwold and Forest Town, taking their names from the Saschenwald 'forest', a vast plantation that once covered the area. This man-made forest was established during the fledgling years of Johannesburg's gold mining era to provide timber for the mine shafts and for construction. These days, only a few isolated pockets remain.

ABOVE The garden at The Pines features an extraordinary collection of aloes. A stone avenue through the garden reconnects the house to its Victorian-era architecture, a period that saw the emergence of a highly competitive plant-collecting craze among the Victorian elite.

OPPOSITE Along the paths of the Aloe Walk, rare but also common aloes, such as the Prickly Aloe (*Aloe aculeata*), are displayed to be admired. Naturally distributed throughout certain parts of Limpopo, Mpumalanga and further north into Zimbabwe, the Prickly Aloe is distinguishable by its thorny leaves and reddish-orange flowers that bloom in winter.

> "Once we had restored the old flora, we wanted to create a footpath that is quite modern but which spoke to the architecture, so we constructed paths that are typical of the sort of stone paths Baker had done in other houses in the area, and at the Union Buildings in Pretoria, and removed the older ones. We also created more modern narrow paths that wound up the hillside towards the Charlotte Maxeke Academic Hospital by setting gravel into cement, so they would not compete with the earth or the natural stone, yet allow ground covers to tumble over onto them quite naturally."

A new cemented gravel route through the forest was lined with large numbers of indigenous White Stinkwood (*Celtis africana*) and Wild Peach (*Kiggelaria africana*), undergrown by tumbling white-flowered Ribbon Bush (*Hypoestes forskaolii*).

Following the forest restoration, Patrick approached the remainder of the koppie in the style of an English wildflower cottage garden, seeking to celebrate the original Arts and Crafts-style plantings while emphasising the restoration programme with beds of indigenous flowering veld shrubs such as Wild Dagga (*Leonotis leonurus*) and Bush Clematis or Feather Duster (*Clematis villosa*), as well as clusters of Zebra or Spotted Aloe (*Aloe zebrina*) and other succulents that typically grow among granitic rock outcrops.

Paths around the koppie, built from rock excavated on the site, are intended to disappear into the landscaping. Benches, tables and reflection ponds have been placed along the route, allowing the view, and the rare plants, to be enjoyed throughout the year.

OPPOSITE Drooping blush-pink flowers are replaced in autumn by ethereal threads of indigenous Bush Clematis or Feather Duster (*Clematis villosa*), a romantic addition to the English wildflower-inspired koppie garden overlooking the Arcadia buildings.

ABOVE (left to right) *Aloe cryptopoda*; *A. petricola*; *Brunsvigia radulosa*.

THE PINES

A larger focus for Patrick's design in the koppie is to create a symbiotic relationship with the urban wildlife in order to accelerate a process of natural restoration across the ridge. Using bird-driven seed dispersal, made possible by the introduction of indigenous fruit-bearing trees, Patrick has laid the groundwork for a food web that allows local birds to reshape the habitat of the garden by spreading seed across the ridge as they feed and move. Recently, through consultation with neighbours, several private gardens and public parks in the area have begun to introduce similar species on their properties to allow the birds sanctuary. It is Patrick's ultimate hope that a 'bird bridge' might be created throughout the ridge and further onwards, encouraging even more species to settle and flourish.

More recently, the campus has expanded to include the neighbouring property known as The Pines, a heritage-grade stone house designed by JC Watson in 1906. Patrick used the building's formidable structure, along with the Victorian approach to landscaping during the period of its construction, as the inspiration for a new garden that would be introduced around the house. Large sections of rock were excavated and exposed, with dainty ground covers planted in between. A delicate fern grotto, which reinforces the neo-Victorian theme, overlooks the avenue, the curvilinear lawn and a lily pond, while an additional cement and gravel route winds through an arboretum of Highveld trees.

Many wealthy Victorians were avid plant collectors, and Patrick has referenced this by building, over a decade, one of the country's most extensive collections of aloes, containing over 600 different species, some of them vulnerable, like *Aloe thorncroftii*. The collection spans a 20-metre-long stone avenue, and Patrick placed many of the plants in crevices between newly built drystone walls that face the aloe avenue. To add interest, many little-seen species of *Adenium*, *Euphorbia* and *Kalanchoe* are dotted among the aloes.

ABOVE (left and right) Wild Aster (*Felicia filifolia*), also known as Fine-leaved Felicia or Draaibos; Wild Dagga or Lion's Ear (*Leonotis ocymifolia* var. *schinzii*).

OPPOSITE Highveld wildflowers add flashes of colour across the koppie in winter.

That the garden at The Pines connects seamlessly with the original Baker garden at Villa Arcadia is a testament to Patrick's ongoing work across both sites over two decades and the implementation of sympathetic hard landscaping, which is almost invisible.

Paths now wind through the whole property – an extensive walk, but the very gradual incline ensures a gentle meander – passing from domestic gardens to wildflower beds, and through shady woodland that is abundant with wildlife. The experience is a rare slice of nature only a stone's throw from the city centre. For the staff who call the campus their base, the property has become a respite from their daily activities and a convenient space to exercise and meditate during the workday.

The future of the project continues to evolve as new plants are included to expand the biodiversity of the collections, inviting ever greater numbers of birds into the garden to spread these threatened seeds throughout the ridge. Gradually, Patrick's vision for a natural process of restoration is growing at a rate that has rarely been attempted at this scale in urban areas anywhere in this country, perhaps, even, in the world.

ARCADIA'S FIRST STEPS

A charming narrative of Arcadia Villa's garden in its early heyday is captured by Dorothea Fairbridge in her book Gardens of South Africa, *in which Fairbridge recounts her first visit as a guest of Lady Phillips:*

'... as I drove into the entrance court of Villa Arcadia and passed through her house on to the long wide stoep I was again conscious of the sudden throb of surprised delight which held me breathless in the dawn. From the stoep and seen through its columns, the blue line of the Magaliesberg Mountains shut out the distant veld, the wonderful monotonous High Veld through which I had come, and below me, falling sharply away from the stoep and melting into the blue-green eucalyptus of the Saschenwald, stretched a garden of exquisite charm. It is not easy to make a garden in that part of Johannesburg, for the natural structure of the land is rock and kopje, and the rock must be blasted out and the soil carted in if you want to plant trees, and to ensure them long life and prosperity.

In planning the garden of Arcadia, Lady Phillips wisely left the kopjes as she found them, crowned with their native plants and queer edible berries, supplementing these in time with aloes and other native plants and trees. The rock was blasted away and untold wagon-loads of rich earth ridden in, and then the less serious business of the garden began. How well she succeeded in making the desert rejoice and blossom I had not glimpsed, until I stood with her that April morning and looked upon her work, drinking in the perfume from great bushes of Heliotrope which grew below the stoep.

Terrace after terrace lay below us, with flights of steps paved with the accommodating sandstone of the Transvaal, which flakes into flat, irregular slabs, far more easily dealt with than the rounded stones of the Cape. Tall Cypresses marked the line of one terrace, cut in the Italian fashion and flanked by Italian oil jars, in which Fuchsias rioted and gleamed in rich purples and reds and pinks. On another terrace was the Rose Garden – roses come to great perfection in the Transvaal – with paved walks between the beds of Teas and Hybrid Teas, laden with blossoms even at this extreme end of summer.

We turned to the right and I saw, through an exquisite, slender gateway of Venetian ironwork, which ended the long stoep, a narrow stretch of grass as fine as velvet, bordered on either side by a clipped hedge

of *Pittosporum eugenioides*, the most charming of plants for topiary work, for it has shiny, black stems and crinkled leaves of pale green. It is an evergreen of very compact growth, and is, moreover, very difficult to strike, so its beauty is set off by its rarity. At the end of the long grass walk was an alcove formed by clipped Cypresses, in which a group of leaden figures took one back to the gardens of England – a slight effort of imagination converting the Cypresses of the south into the clipped Yews of northern lands.

A little flight of steps nearby led into a small and fragrant herb garden, and here we sat and looked up at the house, which was built by Herbert Baker on the lines of an Italian villa, and is wholly satisfying to the eyes – a testimony to one woman's courage in breaking away from the tradition which has hitherto ordained that South African houses shall be wholly English or wholly Dutch, or unsatisfactory hybrids. Here, on the contrary, is the spirit of Southern Europe, brought into Southern Africa, with triumphant success.

The stoep, and the long pergola that flanks it, were glowing with purple Bougainvillea. The flowers and even the leaves of the plants glittered with intense vividness in the clear brilliant atmosphere of the rain-washed morning. The Hibiscus seems to be more scarlet than scarlet itself, and the leaves of the Loquats and Bamboos looked as if they had been carved from jade. One of the terraces was gay with Michaelmas Daisies, which with the Chrysanthemums and other perennials, grow magnificently in the Transvaal.

For this is the region of summer rains, when there is no drought to parch the flowers and no water famines to reduce the exquisite fine lawns of Florida grass to sunburnt deserts. But there are thunderstorms, sometimes accompanied by hailstorms, which beat the flower beds flat and make the owners of little gardens wish that they had never been born – apparently the only summer foe the Transvaal gardener need dread.

His dry season is the winter, and then the vivid green lawns turn golden and the gardens compose themselves to sleep – unlike the gardens of the Cape, where the first rains of autumn set the sap running and the birds singing in exultation at the renewal of life. If you wish for a perfect garden all the year round, you must have one at the Cape from September to December, one in the Transvaal from December to April, and one in Durban for mid-winter.'

FAIRBRIDGE, D., *GARDENS OF SOUTH AFRICA*.
CAPE TOWN: MASKEW MILLER, 1934.

An extraordinary dedication to conservation and restorative gardening by the founders and team of this project is seeing Patrick's dream of the Arcadia campus' revival coming to life, even in the rocky koppie at the property's highest point, where long-absent species are once again thriving in their natural habitat.

20
VICTORIA YARDS
Lorentzville, Johannesburg

Community • Urban • Potager

Working in collaboration with developer Brian Green of 44 Projects (which has become an important champion of Johannesburg's urban regeneration), as well as community stakeholders, Patrick's work to bring new life to the Victoria Yards in downtown Johannesburg reimagines the idea of a potager (food garden) within an inner-city context. A new chapter for this formerly run-down neighbourhood is beginning.

NAMED THE VICTORIA YARDS URBAN AGRICULTURE PROJECT, the gardens of this sprawling development – which spans several city blocks – have been laid out by Green, Patrick and architect Enrico Daffonchio in partnership with 44 Projects. Together, they set out to honour the original architecture of the precinct, which is largely defined by light-industrial warehouse-style buildings. They connected the spaces between these structures by planting food gardens in the corridors between them as well as in the newly created public spaces.

Although the food gardens are now planted and maintained by the surrounding community, Patrick established the gardens at the outset, ensuring that the survival of the plants would be manageable and successful. Patrick also designed a planting scheme for the beds that incorporates edible flowers, allowing the area to remain colourful and plentiful in all seasons.

Today, the communal spaces and gardens are full of life, and have become a vital meeting point for both neighbourhood residents and visitors who come on weekends to explore the food markets held on site.

Birds, bees and insects have returned, pollinating the food plants and surrounding urban gardens, and ensuring jobs are created and income generated for the local community by making space for urban agriculture. This vision comes closer to realisation with each passing day.

PREVIOUS SPREAD (Left) Set deep within an inner-city area that had been neglected by city officials and corporate neighbours, the Victoria Yards development is bringing new life to the suburb of Lorentzville, glowing green between all the neighbouring buildings. (Right) A number of art and design studios have spaces within the development, and frequently contribute their work to exhibits happening around the project.

OPPOSITE The Victoria Yard gardens have become the softening element that ties the vast development together, with herbs even planted between paving blocks on the pathways.

ABOVE Heirloom varietals of popular fruits and vegetables such as ornamental orange, pomegranates, chillies, aubergines, Cape gooseberries and raspberries, have been interplanted with indigenous perennials that keep the garden feeling alive, no matter the season.

Victoria Yards

OPPOSITE AND ABOVE Fruit trees grow abundantly between the beds, which are maintained in part by the residents and tenants, who often contribute plants of their own, adding to the overall diversity of the site.

ABOVE AND OPPOSITE Concrete paths wind through the beds, where food plants are interplanted with plectranthus and other ornamentals.

21
PENINSULA HOUSE
Llandudno, Cape Town
Detail • Coastal • Intimate

OPPOSITE Hardy low-growing coastal shrubs planted in the more exposed parts of the garden, such as Toothed Othonna (*Othonna dentata*), which is naturally adapted to cope with strong, salt-laden winds, look perfectly at home against the grey granite terraces.

LEFT The compact, terraced site includes formal gardens and a pool terrace from which to enjoy the amazing view, while natural coastal vegetation creates a buffer zone onto the rocks.

Located between the ivory sands of one of Cape Town's most spectacular beaches and the coastal fynbos of Table Mountain National Park, a private garden built over and around granite boulders blends elements of a traditional formal garden with the charm of a rustic coastal bolthole.

PATRICK DESCRIBES THE GARDEN, completed in 2015, as a 'jewel box' of delicate, flowering plants – a tribute to one of the homeowners, who has a particular love for the intricate detail of haute couture and fine jewellery.

ABOVE AND OPPOSITE Secluded patios and terraces are planted with beds of hardy shrubs and flowering plants, often surrounded by clipped hedges. In spring, the star-shaped flowers of exotic Frangipani (*Plumeria rubra*) scent the evening air.

The site's extraordinary location posed a challenge, as the steep slope required significant demolition to create space for the home, designed by architect Keith Mason. From a landscaping perspective, exposure to fierce salt-laden winds limited the planting palette considerably.

But challenges often provide unique opportunities. Demolition created an abundance of granite rock that Patrick would utilise as the base material for the landscape design. Working with Mason, Patrick used the rock and rubble to create a series of stepped terraces, each of which has been landscaped 'with its own personality,' he explains.

From intimate courtyards to lawns for sunbathing, the project set out to create unique environments for the owners. Many of the spaces are enclosed by towering stone walls plugged with local succulents, creating green moments throughout the property.

Innovative use of hardy indigenous shrubs, such as Dune Crowberry (*Searsia crenata*), creates hedges that evoke a feeling of formalism, while succulents that tumble over walls give a feeling of lush abundance, meeting the client's challenging brief while staying sensitive to the breathtaking natural environment that surrounds the property.

22
SAXON HOTEL, VILLAS AND SPA
Sandhurst, Johannesburg

Parkland • Rock • Formal

The Saxon Hotel, Villas and Spa is an oasis of tranquillity in the midst of Johannesburg's tree-lined northern suburbs. Spanning some four hectares, the gardens present a minimalist planting palette that sets the tone for the ultimate in rest and relaxation. Designed in the early 2000s, this was one of the first gardens in what would soon become an ongoing partnership between Patrick and insurance entrepreneur Douw Steyn, who once called the Saxon his primary residence. This garden went on to establish a style for their future projects, with the emphasis on texture rather than colour in the plantings.

ABOVE Rolling lawns draw the eye towards shady glades, where White Stinkwoods (*Celtis africana*) are planted among mondo grass.

OPPOSITE Sandstone boulders add both sculptural form and colour to the minimalist green palette used throughout the gardens.

REPEATEDLY VOTED AS ONE of the world's leading boutique hotels, the Saxon understands the importance of providing guests with a memorable experience from arrival to departure. To this end, the gardens offer space for relaxation at the end of a long day of sightseeing or business, and an escape from the city environs. From the terrace, an infinity pool extends onto a lush lawn surrounded by mature trees, underpinned by mounds of ground covers and shade-loving plants.

Beneath the trees, a path invites guests to take a stroll, perhaps to visit the well-tended kitchen garden, where the chefs pick a selection of fresh vegetables and herbs for the day's menus. As you sip a cocktail on the sunset terrace, the mint in your mojito was probably grown on the property, contributing zero carbon miles but scoring high on the satisfaction meter.

As the Saxon Hotel has grown, and other joint projects have been developed, Patrick and Douw Steyn have created an approach that reconsiders European 'formal' landscape design in local situations. They do this by replacing northern hemisphere plants that are trained into hedges and planted in strict symmetry, with indigenous species that are controlled by careful maintenance schedules. These create the same sense of order found in the formal gardens that are often requested by Patrick's clients.

OPPOSITE Massive *Ficus* species grow profusely around the arrival and departure areas, allowing for privacy and creating a sense of escape into a suburban forest.

ABOVE A koi pond provides flashes of colour and a sense of gentle movement beneath the canopy of trees that surround the buildings.

Saxon Hotel, Villas and Spa

ABOVE Guests arrive at the Saxon Hotel via a lengthy driveway that follows a 'scenic route' through the landscape, establishing a sense of place before even reaching the front door.

OPPOSITE Overall, the intention behind the garden design was to establish the concept of a parkland, with wide open lawns and shady tree areas.

Saxon Hotel, Villas and Spa 273

23
SCARBOROUGH HOUSE
Scarborough, Cape Town
Quaint • Fynbos • Coastal

For Patrick, small gardens are no less of a design exercise than his larger projects, and it is important for him to apply the same effort in realising more intimate spaces as he does with larger commissions. In this quaint garden, situated in Scarborough, an artistic village in the 'deep south' of the Cape Peninsula, he has made use of every available space, working with both the architect and the homeowners to extend balcony spaces, terraces and even the underside of staircases to expand the garden throughout the property.

LIKE MANY COASTAL VILLAGES, Scarborough experiences the full force of the wind, from winter's northwesterly gales blowing straight off the Atlantic to summer southeasters that can rapidly strip plants of moisture. This close to the sea, garden plants need to be hardy and well adapted. Fortunately, the Cape coastal region is rich in plant diversity, so Patrick was able to select small trees, shrubs, restios and low-growing ground covers that are capable of withstanding the long dry summers and strong, often salt-laden winds.

The compact, sloping site has been carefully planted so as not to obscure the view, while also providing privacy and protection from the wind. Ground covers tumble naturally over rocks and rockeries, while on the deck, a cleverly placed planter adds softness and texture to the otherwise linear lines of the architecture.

PREVIOUS SPREAD Wind-resistant Coastal Camphor Bush (*Tarchonanthus littoralis*) flanks the entrance to this coastal home, where the use of natural boulders, stone walls, weathered wooden fences and pebble-inlaid concrete emphasises the property's largely unspoilt setting.

THIS SPREAD Alongside the house, large tubs hold hardy Spekboom (*Portulacaria afra*), a popular choice in coastal gardens. The fleshy leaves are both drought- and fire-resistant, an important factor in an area where wind-driven blazes are a constant threat.

PATRICK WATSON
Biographical sketch

PERSONAL LIFE

Born in Johannesburg on 12 March 1947 to James and Laetitia Watson, Patrick is their only son. He has two sisters, Olivia Burdett-Coutts (b. 1945) and Nerine Watson (1949–2006). Watson's father, James, was an architect associated with the Witwatersrand modernist school who had professional partnerships with Rex Martienssen (1905–1942) and John Fassler (1910–1971). His mother was a keen gardener and many of Patrick's ancestors were botanists and nurserymen. The Watson family lived in Bryanston, a rural suburb in the 1950s. Patrick attended school in Johannesburg and, even while at primary school, his family and friends were impressed by his ability to recall and record plants and wildlife.

In October 1980 he married Beryl Behrendt (1950–2018). They had two children, Jean-Paul Watson (b. 1987), who works in property development and landscaping, and Domonique A. James Watson (1989–2022), an artist and art director for television and cinema productions. Beryl and Patrick divorced in 1993 but remained living together for several years thereafter and neither of them remarried.

Patrick, aged 9, holding an owl, photographed by his father, James Watson, at his childhood home in Bryanston. (*Image courtesy Watson archive*)

Influential landscape architect Joane Pim in one of her gardens in Welkom. Pim was an important influence on Patrick's career and his approach to landscape architecture. (*Image courtesy Brenthurst Library*)

EARLY CAREER (1963–1980)

After leaving school, and with his father's encouragement, Patrick considered becoming an architect and worked in Johannesburg as an office assistant to Hellmut Stauch (1910–1970), an architect in the vanguard of innovative European architecture. John Fassler, then Professor of Architecture at the University of the Witwatersrand and a mentor to Patrick, had facilitated the introduction. However, Patrick's interest in plants persisted, and during this time he made regular seed-collecting expeditions across southern Africa with Bea Thompson, founder of Witkoppen Wildflower Nursery – one of the country's first nurseries for exclusively indigenous plants. Thompson became an important figure in Patrick's career, encouraging him to follow his interest in plants and wildlife, and employing him during weekends at her nursery.

Within a year, Patrick had abandoned any desire to become an architect and was employed full-time by Ferndale Ridge Nurseries. He recalls this period as an invaluable experience in understanding client briefs and needs, as well as learning domestic plant behaviour.

Working in the horticultural industry brought him into contact with the highly regarded landscape architect Joane Pim (1904–1974). Her work on the Oppenheimer gardens at Brenthurst in Johannesburg, as well as in the Free State mining town of Welkom, were inspirations to the young man. She gave him guidance and also an introduction that led to his apprenticeship, in 1969, with the extraordinary landscape architect Ann Sutton (1924–2011), whom he assisted with on-the-ground work, drafting plans for her office and managing her site plant lists.

The start of Patrick's career in landscape architecture and design occurred at an exciting time for this profession in South Africa. Until 1971 there had been no formal training or

Pioneering landscape architects Wim Tijmens and Ann Sutton. (*Image courtesy Sutton family*)

qualification in the discipline, but the country's economy was booming and there were many interesting projects in progress that attracted dynamic and creative people. One mega-construction project that included landscaping was the then controversial Rand Afrikaans University in Johannesburg (after 2009 the University of Johannesburg). The young architect Wilhelm Meyer (1935–2006) had been appointed design leader of this huge undertaking and Patrick began working with Meyer on what was an unusual design concept.

In addition to fresh thinking around landscape architecture, the 1970s were a time of new developments in urban design and 'Green' thinking. Patrick's home town of Sandton, founded in 1969 and now integrated into the City of Johannesburg, was one example. Sandton's town council planned river trails, numerous bird sanctuaries and small wildlife reserves. The advice of the Sandton Nature Conservation Society, of which Patrick was a member, was taken seriously. While working for Meyer, he joined a Sandton municipal committee, collaborating with neighbouring local authorities, to conserve the many streams that flow through greater Johannesburg, while also campaigning for the use of more indigenous plants in public infrastructure projects.

Having gained valuable drafting experience during his time with Sutton and Meyer, Patrick joined landscape architects Ben Farrell and Roelf Botha (b. 1933) in Pretoria. The two had formed a partnership to landscape the grounds of Potchefstroom University (reconstituted in 2004 as part of North West University) and Patrick spearheaded the landscaping layouts – one of the largest indigenous planting projects of its time.

Matters were moving ahead quickly in South African landscape architecture and Patrick, as a young newcomer, was in a position to take advantage of them. In 1962 Botha had co-founded the Institute for Landscape Architecture in South Africa (ILASA) together with Joane Pim, Ann Sutton and Peter Leutscher, which became affiliated to the International Federation of Landscape Architects. A further important step towards full professionalisation came in 1971 when a Chair of Landscape Architecture was created at the University of Pretoria. The year 1973 was important in the evolution of the local landscape design community and also in Patrick's career. With a well-established institute and a formal academic department, the stage was set for the first landscape architecture conference to be held in South Africa. The theme of the inaugural conference, which took place at the University of South Africa in Pretoria, was 'Planning for Environmental Conservation'. Leading international figures attended, including famous personalities such as Ian McHarg (1920–2001), founder of the Department of Landscape Architecture at the University of Pennsylvania, whose seminal book *Design with Nature* (1969) was a significant influence on Patrick's thinking. There was also a presentation by eminent and influential Brazilian landscaper and artist Roberto Burle Marx (1909–1994) who had pioneered fresh ideas around design. Burle Marx and Patrick became friends almost immediately, leading to a long-lasting creative professional relationship.

Roberto Burle Marx, Ian McHarg, Joane Pim, Ann Sutton and other leaders of the landscaping community photographed at the inaugural conference of the Institute for Landscape Architecture in South Africa, held in 1973 at the University of South Africa. (*Image courtesy Fassler Collection, University of Pretoria*)

Roberto Burle Marx shows Patrick around Sítio, the pioneering and eccentric landscaper's vast estate in Rio de Janeiro, Brazil, which was inscribed in 2021 on the UNESCO World Heritage List. (*Image courtesy Fassler Collection, University of Pretoria*)

The conference heralded Patrick's initial endeavours towards a solo career. His first professional commission came a year later, when he created the gardens for the new corporate head office of MSD Pharmaceuticals in Midrand, Gauteng. After the conference, he accompanied Burle Marx on a tour around South Africa so the visitor might see the plants and wildlife, as well as meet leading local landscaping figures, something Burle Marx would reciprocate on Patrick's many later visits to Brazil.

At the time, Patrick was assisting Sydney Press (1919–1997), founder of Edgars Consolidated Stores, to establish a nursery on his family farm near Lydenburg (now Mashishing, Mpumalanga). The house had been designed by Marco Zanuso (1916–2001), a leader in the Italian-led international movement for 'good design'. The architecture of the new dwelling was intimately connected to the surrounding landscape, even including an earth roof. Patrick followed Zanuso's lead, devising a planting scheme that recreated the surrounding habitat. He began the enterprise by establishing a nursery for plants grown from seed collected on the site. Patrick and Burle Marx had originally developed a joint proposal for the overall landscaping for the farm, named 'Coromandel', but Press rejected it, and instead worked with Patrick alone.

In 1976 Sydney Press introduced Patrick to Isador Baba Selsick (b. 1955), an architect responsible for many of the design icons of South Africa. This led to a major commission – still ongoing – to landscape Sun City Hotel, in a region that was about to transform from an apartheid 'Bantustan' into 'independent' Bophuthatswana. Selsick put him in touch with Sol Kerzner (1935–2020), the visionary founder of the Sun International hotel group. It was to become a lasting collaboration. In Kerzner, Patrick found a patron and client who recognised his talents and allowed him to express his creativity fully. Over almost two decades, Patrick has designed the landscaping across the Sun City Hotel and Casino resort, an area of some 30,000 hectares, that eventually included the Palace of the Lost City, Lost City Gardens, Lost City Golf Course and Valley of the Waves. In addition, he has designed a score of other Sun International projects in southern Africa and the Indian Ocean islands, working across South Africa, Zimbabwe, Seychelles, Comoros, Mauritius and Mozambique.

THE GRAND TOURS (1981–1999)

Patrick's contracts with Sydney Press at Coromandel Farm, Edgardale, and the family estate in Johannesburg were informal. There was no agreed budget or arrangements for payment. The two negotiated an imaginative means of recompense: support for international travel, a 'Grand Tour', that would further Patrick's design education. In 1981, he first visited Burle Marx in Brazil, exploring his gardens, and the forests around Rio de Janeiro. He then travelled on to Venezuela and thereafter to the United States, visiting Miami, Dallas, Las Vegas, Los Angeles and Portland, as well as the states of Georgia, Arizona and Hawaii. Then came Asia, with visits to Japan, China, Sri Lanka and parts of India.

Travelling with this purpose enabled Patrick to meet leading architects and designers in the USA, including Michael Graves (1934–2015), who familiarised him with the work of both Frank Lloyd Wright (1862–1959) and Louis Kahn (1901–1974), and the buildings and gardens of other prominent international design figures. Some years later, Patrick entered into a similar arrangement with a different client, enabling him to tour historic gardens and architectural sites throughout Europe and the United Kingdom with Beryl, soaking up centuries of design inspiration from noteworthy gardens and great estates.

These 'grand tours' provided creative direction at a time when his projects were happening faster and were getting larger. The experiences liberated him to explore new international styles and to experiment with different historical techniques. These have ranged from minimalist landscapes that echo Frank Lloyd Wright's early work with local rock, such as the landscape created for the Saxon Hotel in Johannesburg, to projects that explore fantasy and excess, similar to some of the landscapes he saw in the Americas. His travels gave him the confidence to take big decisions in short timelines and allowed him to become evermore ambitious with the scope and scale of his briefs and his vision.

Coromandel Farm, near Lydenburg (now Mashishing). (*Image courtesy M. Courtney Clarke/David Goldblatt*)

Patrick (far left), Sydney Press, Marco Zanuso and Victoria Press. (*Image courtesy Suzanne Press & Associates*)

Designed by architect Marco Zanuso, the gardens at Coromandel Farm, near Lydenburg (now Mashishing), were one of Patrick's first landscaping commissions, and the first project that required the establishment of a dedicated on-site nursery – something that has come to inform the process of Patrick's design approach ever since. (*Images courtesy M. Courtney Clarke/David Goldblatt*)

One of the techniques devised by Patrick when working on large-scale projects is to throw hundreds of coloured sticks across the property, each colour representing a different plant on his list. The corresponding specimens are then planted where the sticks have landed, thereby simulating the appearance of randomness in a natural landscape. The technique, seen here at Sun City Hotel, continues to evolve as Patrick's legacy projects develop into their next phases. (*Image courtesy Dave Kirkby/Top Turf archive*)

LEGACY PROJECTS (1999–CURRENT)

Since the start of his career, many of Patrick's projects have exceeded the scale of typical landscaping ventures. Many have required sustained attention; some, like Sun City, continuing for over four decades under his guidance. Later undertakings have included Steyn City, a vast parkland development by insurance magnate Douw Steyn, for which Patrick established dedicated nurseries a decade before the project even broke ground. However, it is a mark of his extraordinary versatility that he is also able to assist many private clients who have far smaller gardens and fewer resources, ensuring that his talent has been widely appreciated. Every project, whether large or small, is given equal attention and his unique creativity.

But it is what he calls 'legacy projects' that have come to define much of Patrick's oeuvre, and they continue to expand in scope. He has developed remarkably ambitious nurseries for many of his works, including Sun City, Steyn City and island projects such as those in the Seychelles, Mauritius, and São Tomé and Príncipe. While these nurseries are rarely seen by the public it is they, and the people he has trained, that sustain maintenance and expansion.

As Patrick's projects – and his own outlook – have evolved, he has moved closer towards working with the natural environment, allowing plants to self-seed and increase their impact to conserve and restore landscapes beyond the time horizon of the project itself. Thanks to this sort of 'future-proof' planning, projects such as those at Arcadia in Johannesburg and North Island in the Seychelles, among others, can look ahead to a time when Patrick himself will no longer be physically present to craft the landscape or create the conditions for natural ecological systems, yet they will continue to sustain themselves and flourish.

ABOVE A project by the same developers as Sun City, the Kingdom Hotel at Victoria Falls, Zimbabwe (which, at the time of publication, had closed its doors) looked towards indigenous species that could create a similar sense of fantasy as that achieved in the Lost City gardens. (*Image Ariadne Van Zandbergen/Alamy Stock Photo*)

LEFT Situated on the forested banks of the Zambezi River in Zambia, overlooking the majestic, thundering waters of Mosi-oa-Tunya (Victoria Falls), Patrick's original landscaping for the grounds of the historic Royal Livingstone Hotel (now Avani Victoria Falls Resort) appear as if they have always been there. (*Image courtesy Avani Victoria Falls Resort*)

OPPOSITE On a 2022 trip to Mauritius, Patrick revisited several projects that have been completed by his team over two decades across the island, including Mont Choisy, Le Coco Beach, Sugar Beach Resort, Le Touessrok and several others. These legacy projects continue to develop, some with his assistance, and some without, self-seeding as their message and vision continue to grow. (*Images courtesy Patrick Watson/ Domonique A. James Watson*)

THE GARDENER'S GARDEN

Greenside, Johannesburg

Collections • Rewilding • Timeless

Sitting at a table in his home in Greenside, Johannesburg, where he has lived for three decades, Patrick discusses his life, and how he found his love for plants. Before settling in for our discussion, he explains that he sees the garden surrounding the house – an eclectic forest that threatens to take over the building – as 'a plant orphanage', a place where specimens removed from projects during demolition, salvaged from building sites, or saved from homes he has lived in, can find sanctuary. Here, exotics grow alongside indigenous plants, succulents emerge from beneath ferns, and cacti dangle from tree branches, everything thriving in perfect chaos and harmony – a place that is alive with suburban birdlife and his beloved dogs.

Garreth You've said before that you started gardening seriously when you were six…

Patrick I think even earlier, quite frankly. You know, all kids garden, planting little flowers here and there, but I obviously carried on more seriously. After a few years, my childhood friends moved on to bicycles, girls and then sports cars, but I've always been happy with the veld, and my dogs. I grew up in Bryanston, where there were very few houses in the 1950s. It was just veld everywhere, like living on a farm, and I would walk with my parents every day. You'd see jackal, steenbok, snakes, chameleons – just fantastic to grow up with, really. My father was very keen on plants. He liked climbing mountains, and plants, and natural things, but in an amateur way. He was an architect, and my mother was a keen amateur gardener.

ABOVE SEQUENCE Enormous euphorbias, grown from small plants, and aloes collected from various projects, tell the story of Patrick's landscaping career and personal life at his home in Greenside, Johannesburg.

RIGHT Plants collected over three decades find sanctuary in Patrick's garden, where indigenous and exotic plants from his life and projects live among one another.

Of course, I didn't know about any of that at the time. I really don't think the walks, or their influence, made me want to do this. I just wanted to do it, and I think it's about genetics.

I see it now with my son, Jean-Paul, who is starting to design his own gardens, and his natural knack for it, and how it has been a big interest in many of his ancestors, and mine, so I think genetics play an important part in these sorts of decisions. My father planted a little veld garden at our house, which was unusual at that time, and all of his friends were interested in these sorts of things as well, like his business partner Harold Porter, after whom the Harold Porter National Botanical Garden is named, and we spent a lot of time together. I remember walking with him around the Portersfield Estate in Betty's Bay, which became the Botanical Garden, but I already knew a lot of the plants we were seeing even then, and I must've only been nine years old at the time. He died the next year, and I got to know his wife very well later. So we were always mixed up with people like that, but I was always obsessed with biodiversity, really, and took it on myself.

Garreth Your parents' garden sounds beautiful.
Patrick It was really something, when I look back on it. It had these wide lawns, and a big vegetable garden, and then my father planted the veld garden. He certainly had a talent for it, and would've made a good landscape architect if there was such a thing at the time. But we grew up in the veld at a time when Jo'burg was covered in bush and rock outcrops and clumps of trees, and then there was the city going up around

The gardener's garden

you, which is what I think I like about gardens on the Highveld. They grow between these really industrialised landscapes. The mine dumps and factories are contrasted with this quite wild nature, so when you make something here there is this sort of land art that happens around you all the time, where the mine dumps make mounds and mountains of veld, and that rubs off on you when you grow up here, and your idea of nature.

Garreth What was school like for you?

Patrick Honestly, I never took a serious interest in it. My sister did very well, top of the class, best at sport, but I found it very boring. But I have always been really interested in reading, and passionate about it. I remember going with my mother to buy a book when I was about four or five and telling her that I wanted 'a true book', because I've never really liked fiction. Of course I enjoyed stories like *Alice in Wonderland* and *Lord of The Rings*, especially when it comes to landscape design, but I like facts most of all. I've always had this obsession with reason, and I think education at the time was really by roto, and I couldn't understand it. My own kids had a different education. But what I understand, I understand, and what I don't, I delegate, and it's how I have managed to get things done, otherwise I wouldn't get all these jobs done. But I read for at least four hours a day, if not more. On weekends, I never stop: watching, reading.

Garreth As someone who hardly exercises I can barely keep up with you! When we walk through the gardens together, your pace is honestly herculean. But I remember walking with you through the park the other day and noticing how you weren't just looking at plants, but looking at what grew alongside them, or near them, and how close this one was to the water, or that one on a hill.

Patrick The truth is I only climb mountains to see what plants are on top. I certainly don't do it for the exercise. When I'm walking, I collect seeds, or garden plants that I might use, but it's not always about gardens. You have to understand ecology, how nature works, how it all fits together, all the little pieces, to do this job. It's why at Steyn City, where I planted those wild trees, they are now seeding themselves. If someone had planted them atop a hill, or on a beach, they wouldn't seed themselves. So it's about sustainability, but I'm also interested in aesthetics, about things being in their right place. You need to know in your mind if it's a grey garden, or a green garden, or a red garden, or this or that, and then you put it in like a computer. I have a very mechanical brain actually. But it's all about concept for me. I'm conceptual, I like a concept, and I get a concept. Nature's a concept. Seychelles, for instance, is a concept. The desert is a concept. Fynbos is a concept. Designers must ask, is it a classical concept? Is it grey, is it indigenous, or a nature park, or not. So you put all these things into your little computer, and you come up with a solution. But

beneath it all, you have to know your plants, know that some ferns grow in water and some ferns grow in the desert. If you don't know your plants, you are just wasting your time. A client asked me about Bobbejaansterts, also known as Black-stick Lily (*Xerophyta retinervis*), plants that are, like, 300 years old in the wild, and you have to remove all the soil with them or they won't make it. So you need to know your plants, or things die, but it's also about instinct.

I think instinct has a lot to do with gardening, because it's too complicated if you don't work with your instinct. But still, it helps to see it in nature, because then you know. There are reasons for things, and you need to meditate on them. If you choose to work on instinct though, then you need to be dead serious. It's what the Romans called 'gravitas'. You must think and act like it's life or death, in the decisions you make, or otherwise it's a serious problem.

If you think it's just a game then you are going to make serious mistakes. The best leaders are always more or less instinctive, but for many, their egos get the best of them. Once you have an ego that believes you're wonderful and that you can't go wrong, then you're going to go wrong. Like a good artist, they just paint. That's why I don't like to draw too much. Once you get into it, the thing evolves, and it suddenly comes

2
SPIER ESTATE

1. Coral Tree (*Erythrina lysistemon*) | 2. African Lily (*Agapanthus africanus*)

FARM ESTATE

Adiantum capillus-veneris
Adiantum spp.
Afrocanthium mundianum
Agapanthus africanus
Agapanthus praecox
Agathosma spp.
Aloe arborescens
Aloe microstigma subsp. *microstigma*
Aloe succotrina
Aloiampelos commixta
Amaryllis belladonna
Ammocharis longifolia
Andropogon eucomus
Apodytes dimidiata
Aponogeton angustifolius
Aponogeton distachyos
Arctopus spp.
Arctotheca spp.
Arctotis spp.
Aristea capitata
Aristea thyrsiflora
Athanasia crithmifolia
Athanasia dentata
Babiana nervosa
Baeometra uniflora
Ballota africana
Berzelia lanuginosa
Blechnum attenuatum
Bonatea speciosa
Brabejum stellatifolium
Brachylaena neriifolia
Brunsvigia orientalis
Bulbine alooides
Bulbine praemorsa
Bulbinella floribunda
Carex aethiopica
Carpobrotus acinaciformis
Carpobrotus edulis
Cassine papillosa
Celtis africana
Cenchrus caudatus
Centella asiatica
Chasmanthe aethiopica
Chironia baccifera
Chironia linoides
Chrysocoma cernua
Cineraria geifolia
Cladium mariscus
Clematis brachiata
Colchicum capense
Colchicum eucomoides
Cotula coronopifolia
Tylecodon grandiflorus
Cotyledon orbiculata
Crassula muscosa
Crassula natans
Crassula nudicaulis
Crassula pellucida
Crinum longifolium
Crossyne guttata
Crotalaria capensis
Cunonia capensis
Curtisia dentata
Cyanella hyacinthoides
Cysticapnos vesicaria
Dicerothamnus rhinocerotis
Dimorphotheca fruticosa
Dimorphotheca pluvialis
Diospyros whyteana
Dodonaea viscosa
Dorotheanthus bellidiformis
Drosanthemum floribundum
Empodium plicatum
Eragrostis curvula
Erepsia anceps
Erica baccans
Erica caffra
Erica cerinthoides
Erica coccinea
Erica curviflora
Erica imbricata
Erica plukenetii
Erica sessiliflora
Erythrina lysistemon
Euclea racemosa
Euclea tomentosa
Euphorbia caput-medusae
Euphorbia mauritanica
Falkia repens
Felicia amelloides
Felicia fruticosa
Ferraria crispa
Gazania pinnata
Geranium incanum
Grewia occidentalis
Grielum grandiflorum
Gunnera perpensa
Gymnosporia acuminata
Gymnosporia buxifolia
Haemanthus coccineus
Hemarthria altissima
Halleria elliptica
Halleria lucida
Hemimeris racemosa
Hemimeris sabulosa
Hermannia alnifolia
Hermas villosa
Ilex mitis
Imperata cylindrica
Kiggelaria africana
Kniphofia uvaria
Knowltonia capensis
Knowltonia vesicatoria
Lasiospermum bipinnatum
Lemna gibba
Leonotis leonurus
Lessertia frutescens
Leucadendron argenteum
Leucadendron salignum
Leucospermum conocarpodendron subsp. *conocarpodendron*
Maurocenia frangula
Maytenus acuminata
Moraea bellendenii
Moraea fugax
Moraea neglecta
Moraea ramosissima
Moraea setifolia
Moraea tripetala
Moraea tristis
Muraltia heisteria
Muraltia spinosa
Myrica quercifolia
Myrica serrata
Myrsine africana
Myrsine melanophloeos
Myrsine pillansii
Nerine sarniensis
Noltea africana
Notobubon galbaniopse
Nymphaea nouchali var. *nouchali*
Ocotea bullata
Oedera capensis
Oedera imbricata
Oftia africana
Olea capensis
Olea europaea subsp. *cuspidata*
Olinia ventosa
Orphium frutescens
Osmitopsis asteriscoides

Osmitopsis dentata
Osyris lanceolata
Othonna dentata
Othonna quinquedentata
Oxalis bifida
Paspalum vaginatum
Passerina filiformis
Pauridia aquatica
Pauridia capensis
Pelargonium alchemilloides
Pelargonium betulinum
Pelargonium cucullatum
Pelargonium myrrhifolium
Pellaea hastata
Phylica buxifolia
Podalyria calyptrata
Podalyria sericea
Podocarpus latifolius
Potamogeton pusillus
Prionium serratum
Protea coronata
Protea cynaroides
Protea grandiceps
Protea grandiflora
Protea lepidocarpodendron
Protea neriifolia
Protea pulchella
Protea repens
Protea speciosa
Pteridium aquilinum
Putterlickia pyracantha
Rhamnus prinoides
Rubus rigidus
Salix babylonica
Salix mucronata
Salvia africana
Salvia chamelaeagnea
Scolopia mundii
Scutia myrtina
Searsia angustifolia
Searsia crenata
Searsia glauca
Searsia incana
Searsia lucida
Searsia pyroides
Searsia rosmarinifolia
Secamone alpini
Sideroxylon inerme
Sium spp.
Sparaxis elegans
Sparaxis grandiflora
Stachys aethiopica
Stuckenia pectinata
Syzygium cordatum
Tarchonanthus camphoratus
Tecomaria capensis
Trachyandra ciliata
Trachyandra divaricata
Tritonia crocata
Vachellia karroo
Veltheimia bracteata
Veltheimia capensis
Vepris lanceolata
Virgilia oroboides
Wachendorfia paniculata
Wachendorfia thyrsiflora
Watsonia aletroides
Watsonia angusta
Watsonia borbonica
Watsonia galpinii
Watsonia knysnana
Watsonia laccata
Watsonia marginata
Watsonia meriana
Watsonia spectabilis
Watsonia vanderspuyae
Widdringtonia nodiflora
Wurmbea stricta
Zantedeschia aethiopica
Ziziphus mucronata
   subsp. *mucronata*

VELD

Albuca canadensis
Aloe mitriformis
Aponogeton distachyos
Arctotheca calendula
Arctotis acaulis
Babiana angustifolia
Babiana melanops
Babiana nervosa
Babiana ringens
Babiana rubrocyanea
Babiana tubiflora
Babiana tubulosa
Brunsvigia elandsmontana
Bulbinella nutans subsp. *nutans*
Dicerothamnus rhinocerotis
Dimorphotheca pluvialis
Dimorphotheca sinuata
Erica cerinthoides
Erica jasminiflora
Erica mammosa
Eriocephalus africanus
Eriocephalus racemosus
Euclea racemosa subsp. *racemosa*
Geissorhiza aspera
Gladiolus alatus
Gladiolus angustus
Gladiolus carinatus
Gladiolus carneus
Gladiolus liliaceus
Gladiolus watsonius
Hermannia alnifolia
Hyobanche sanguinea
Hyparrhenia hirta
Ixia maculata
Ixia scillaris subsp. *scillaris*
Kiggelaria africana
Kniphofia uvaria
Lachenalia aloides
Lachenalia pallida
Leonotis leonurus
Lessertia frutescens
Liparia splendens subsp. *splendens*
Lobostemon fruticosus
Microloma tenuifolium
Moraea bellendenii
Moraea bifida
Moraea elegans
Moraea fugax
Moraea gawleri
Moraea villosa
Moraea villosa
   subsp. *elandsmontana*
Moraea villosa subsp. *villosa*
Nerine sarniensis
Olea europaea
   subsp. *cuspidata*
Orbea pulchella
Ornithogalum thyrsoides
Pauridia capensis
Pelargonium capitatum
Pelargonium myrrhifolium
   var. *myrrhifolium*
Pelargonium peltatum

Podocarpus elongatus
Protea cynaroides
Themeda triandra
Wachendorfia paniculata
Watsonia borbonica
Watsonia marginata
Watsonia meriana
Wurmbea stricta
Zantedeschia aethiopica

RIVERSIDE

Andropogon appendiculatus
Andropogon eucomus
   subsp. *huillensis*
Aponogeton distachyos
Bolboschoenus maritimus
Capeochloa cincta subsp. *cincta*
Carex clavata
Carpha glomerata
Cenchrus caudatus
Cenchrus geniculatus
Cladium mariscus subsp. *jamaicense*
Cyperus congestus
Cyperus denudatus
Cyperus fastigiatus
Cyperus laevigatus
Cyperus longus subsp. *longus*
Cyperus mundii
Cyperus nitidus
Cyperus textilis
Echinochloa crus-galli
Elegia capensis
Eleocharis dregeana
Eleocharis limosa
Ficinia nodosa
Fuirena hirsuta
Hemarthria altissima
Imperata cylindrica
Isolepis prolifera
Isolepis setacea
Juncus dregeanus subsp. *dregeanus*
Juncus effusus
Juncus lomatophyllus
Juncus oxycarpus
Juncus rigidus
Miscanthus ecklonii
Nymphaea nouchali var. *caerulea*
Nymphoides thunbergiana
Paspalum distichum
Paspalum vaginatum
Phragmites australis
Polypogon viridis
Potamogeton nodosus
Prionium serratum
Protea burchellii
Protea coronata
Protea repens
Pseudoschoenus inanis
Schoenoplectus tabernaemontani
Stenotaphrum dimidiatum
Tetraria secans
Xyris capensis

3
DARAHEEN FARM

1. Wild Dagga (*Leonotis leonurus*) | 2. Giant Honey Flower (*Melianthus major*)

Adromischus sphenophyllus
Agathosma capensis
Agathosma ovata
Albuca canadensis
Albuca juncifolia
Aloe buhrii
Aloe comosa
Aloe cooperi
Aloe falcata
Aloe kouebokkeveldensis
Aloe perfoliata
Amaryllis belladonna
Arctotis acaulis
Arctotis calendula
Arctotis incisa
Aristea africana
Aristea capitata
Aristida junciformis
Asparagus capensis
Asparagus lignosus
Asparagus spp.
Asparagus virgatus
Athanasia dentata
Athanasia trifurcata
Athanasia vestita
Babiana angustifolia
Babiana spp.
Babiana villosa
Berzelia lanuginosa
Bobartia rufa
Brabejum stellatifolium
Brachylaena neriifolia
Brianhuntleya purpureostyla
Brunsvigia bosmaniae
Buddleja saligna
Buddleja salviifolia
Bulbine alooides
Bulbinella nutans
Calodendrum capense
Carpha glomerata
Cassine peragua
Celtis africana
Cenchrus caudatus
Chaenostoma revolutum
Chaenostoma uncinatum
Chasmanthe bicolor
Chasmanthe floribunda
Chasmanthe floribunda
   var. *duckittii*
Chrysocoma ciliaris
Chrysocoma cernua
Cissampelos capensis

Cliffortia ruscifolia
Cliffortia strobilifera
Coleus madagascariensis
Cotyledon orbiculata
Cotyledon spp.
Crassula fallax
Cyanella alba
Cyanella hyacinthoides
Cymbopogon spp.
Cyperus textilis
Dicerothamnus rhinocerotis
Dimorphotheca cuneata
Dimorphotheca pluvialis
Dimorphotheca sinuata
Diospyros glabra
Diospyros whyteana
Dodonaea viscosa
   subsp. *angustifolia*
Dovyalis caffra
Drosanthemum bicolor
Ehrharta calycina
Ehrharta capensis
Ehrharta villosa
Elegia capensis
Elegia fistulosa
Eragrostis curvula
Erepsia aspera
Erica caffra
Erica cerinthoides
Erica curviflora
Erica discolor
Erica grandiflora
Erica inflata
Erica lateralis
Erica mammosa
Erica versicolor
Eriocephalus africanus
   var. *paniculatus*
Eriocephalus ericoides
Eucomis regia
Euphorbia mauritanica
Euryops abrotanifolius
Euryops spp.
Euryops thunbergii
Felicia aethiopica
Felicia filifolia
Felicia heterophylla
Felicia hyssopifolia
Ferraria divaricata
Freesia spp.
Freylinia lanceolata
Freylinia visseri

Gasteria brachyphylla
Gladiolus alatus
Gladiolus carneus
Gnidia oppositifolia
Gnidia squarrosa
Gomphocarpus cancellatus
Gymnosporia buxifolia
Haemanthus coccineus
Halleria elliptica
Halleria lucida
Heeria argentea
Helichrysum aureum
Helichrysum cymosum
Helichrysum dasyanthum
Helichrysum pandurifolium
Helichrysum patulum
Helichrysum teretifolium
Hermannia pinnata
Hermannia saccifera
Hermannia spp.
Homeria spp.
Hymenolepis crithmifolia
Hypodiscus aristatus
Ilex mitis
Ixia dubia
Ixia scillaris subsp. *scillaris*
Ixia viridiflora
Jasminum glaucum
Jasminum grandiflorum
Jasminum multipartitum
Jordaaniella spp.
Kiggelaria africana
Kniphofia sarmentosa
Kniphofia uvaria
Kumara plicatilis
Lachenalia aloides
Lachenalia orchioides
Lampranthus bicolor
Lampranthus emarginatus
Lampranthus glomeratus
Lampranthus hoerleinianus
Lampranthus watermeyeri
Lapeirousia spp.
Leonotis leonurus
Lessertia frutescens
Leucadendron brunioides
Leucadendron chamelaea
Leucadendron corymbosum
Leucadendron lanigerum
   var. *lanigerum*
Leucadendron salignum
Leucadendron tinctum

Leucospermum reflexum
Leucospermum vestitum
Lobostemon argenteus
Lobostemon fruticosus
Maytenus acuminata
Maytenus oleoides
Melianthus major
Melinis repens
Merxmuellera stricta
Metalasia muricata
Metrosideros angustifolia
Micranthus junceus
Mimetes cucullatus
Monopsis lutea
Monsonia speciosa
Montinia caryophyllacea
Moraea maximiliani
Moraea ramosissima
Muraltia heisteria
Muraltia spinosa
Myrsine africana
Nerine sarniensis
Oftia africana
Olea capensis
Olea europaea subsp. *cuspidata*
Olinia ventosa
Orbea variegata
Ornithogalum dubium
Ornithogalum thyrsoides
Osteospermum imbricatum
Osteospermum moniliferum
Osyris compressa
Otholobium decumbens
Oxalis purpurea
Passerina truncata
Pelargonium capense
Pelargonium cucullatum
Pelargonium grandiflorum
Pelargonium magenteum
Pelargonium peltatum
Pelargonium tomentosum
Pelargonium triste
Pentameris airoides
Phylica buxifolia
Phylica ericoides
Phylica oleifolia
Phylica pubescens
Platylophus trifoliatus
Plectranthus ciliatus
Podalyria calyptrata
Podocarpus elongatus
Podocarpus latifolius
Polygala sericea
Printzia aromatica
Prionium serratum
Protea nana
Protea neriifolia
Protea nitida
Protea repens
Psoralea pinnata
Relhania fruticosa
Restio festuciformis
Restio subverticillatus
Rodocoma spp.
Salix mucronata
Salvia africana
Salvia chamelaeagnea
Salvia lanceolata
Scabiosa columbaria
Scabiosa incisa
Scirpus fluitans
Scirpus nodosus
Searsia angustifolia
Searsia crenata
Searsia laevigata
Searsia lucida
Searsia undulata
Selago canescens
Selago corymbosa
Senecio macroglossus
Seriphium plumosum
Serruria pedunculata
Serruria undulata
Sparaxis grandiflora
Staberoha banksii
Stachys aethiopica
Struthiola dodecandra
Tarchonanthus camphoratus
Tetragonia fruticosa
Thamnochortus spicigerus
Thereianthus ixioides
Themeda triandra
Tribolium uniolae
Tulbaghia capensis
Tulista pumila
Tylecodon paniculatus
Ursinia pilifera
Ursinia sericea
Ursinia speciosa
Veltheimia capensis
Virgilia oroboides
Wachendorfia thyrsiflora
Watsonia borbonica
  subsp. *ardernei*
Watsonia meriana

4
MORULENG CULTURAL PRECINCT

1. Marula (*Sclerocarya birrea* subsp. *caffra*) | 2. Bushveld Candelabra Tree (*Euphorbia cooperi*)

Acalypha glabrata var. *glabrata*
Acokanthera oppositifolia
Adansonia digitata
Aloe davyana
Aloe marlothii
Aloe zebrina
Annona senegalensis subsp. *senegalensis*
Artemisia afra
Asparagus laricinus
Asparagus suaveolens
Athrixia elata
Babiana hypogaea
Bauhinia macrantha
Berchemia zeyheri
Boophane disticha
Bowiea volubilis subsp. *volubilis*
Bulbine frutescens
Bulbine narcissifolia
Carissa bispinosa
Carissa spinarum
Cassine transvaalensis
Catharanthus roseus
Celosia argentea
Centella asiatica
Ceropegia crassifolia var. *crassifolia*
Ceropegia nilotica var. *nilotica*
Coccinia mackenii
Combretum apiculatum subsp. *apiculatum*
Combretum hereroense
Combretum imberbe
Commiphora neglecta
Cotyledon orbiculata var. *orbiculata*
Crinum bulbispermum
Crinum macowanii
Croton gratissimus var. *gratissimus*
Cucumis metuliferus
Cucumis myriocarpus
Cucumis zeyheri
Cussonia spicata
Cynanchum viminale subsp. *viminale*
Dioscorea dregeana
Diospyros lycioides subsp. *lycioides*
Diospyros whyteana
Dipcadi viride
Dodonaea viscosa. subsp. *angustifolia*
Dombeya rotundifolia var. *rotundifolia*
Dovyalis caffra
Dovyalis zeyheri
Dracaena aethiopica
Dracaena hyacinthoides
Dracaena pearsonii
Duvalia polita
Ehretia rigida subsp. *nervifolia*
Elaeodendron transvaalense
Entada elephantina
Erythrina lysistemon
Euclea crispa subsp. *crispa*
Euclea natalensis subsp. *natalensis*
Euclea undulata
Eucomis autumnalis
Euphorbia cooperi
Euphorbia ingens
Ficus abutilifolia
Ficus ingens
Ficus salicifolia
Ficus thonningii
Gardenia thunbergia
Gomphocarpus fruticosus subsp. *fruticosus*
Grewia bicolor var. *bicolor*
Grewia flava
Grewia occidentalis var. *occidentalis*
Hemionitis calomelanos
Heteromorpha arborescens var. *abyssinica*
Hilliardiella elaeagnoides
Hoslundia opposita
Hyperacanthus amoenus
Hypoestes forskaolii
Hypoxis hemerocallidea
Hypoxis obtusa
Imperata cylindrica
Ipomoea crassipes var. *crassipes*
Ipomoea oblongata
Jasminum stenolobum
Kirkia wilmsii
Lannea edulis
Lantana rugosa
Lessertia frutescens subsp. *frutescens*
Lippia javanica
Mimusops zeyheri
Olea europaea subsp. *cuspidata*
Opuntia ficus-indica
Pappea capensis
Pavetta gardeniifolia var. *gardeniifolia*
Pelargonium luridum
Phytolacca dioica
Plantago lanceolata
Plumbago auriculata
Portulacaria afra
Rhoicissus tridentata subsp. *tridentata*
Riocreuxia torulosa var. *torulosa*
Scadoxus puniceus
Schotia brachypetala
Sclerocarya birrea subsp. *caffra*
Searsia leptodictya
Searsia pyroides var. *pyroides*
Searsia undulata
Talinum caffrum
Tarchonanthus camphoratus
Terminalia sericea
Tetradenia riparia
Tylosema esculentum
Tylosema fassoglense
Vachellia karroo
Vachellia tortilis subsp. *heteracantha*
Volkameria glabra
Withania somnifera
Ximenia americana
Xysmalobium undulatum var. *undulatum*
Ziziphus mucronata subsp. *mucronata*

5
NORTH ISLAND, SEYCHELLES

1. Takamaka Tree (*Calophyllum inophyllum*) | 2. Wright's Gardenia (*Rothmannia annae*)

In the plantings on North Island, Patrick Watson used tropical species endemic to the Seychelles and other Indian Ocean Islands. The species listed below therefore do not appear on the South African National Plant Checklist published by SANBI but are listed in the database of Plants of the World Online, managed by Royal Botanic Gardens, Kew.

Allophylus pervillei
Allophylus sechellensis
Aphloia theiformis
Averrhoa bilimbi
Barringtonia asiatica
Barringtonia racemosa
Calophyllum inophyllum
Carissa spinarum
Cerbera manghas
Colea seychellarum
Colubrina asiatica
Cordia subcordata
Deckenia nobilis
Dodonaea viscosa
Dracaena reflexa
Euphorbia pyrifolia
Excoecaria spp.
Ficus bojeri
Ficus lutea
Ficus reflexa
Ficus rubra

Grisollea thomassetii
Guettarda speciosa
Gynura sechellensis
Heliotropium arboreum
Heritiera littoralis
Hernandia nymphaeifolia
Hibiscus tiliaceus
Intsia bijuga
Jatropha curcas
Lodoicea maldivica
Ludia mauritiana
Martellidendron hornei
Mimusops sechellarum
Nephrosperma vanhoutteanum
Northia seychellana
Ochrosia oppositifolia
Pandanus balfourii
Pandanus multispicatus
Pandanus sechellarum
Paragenipa lancifolia
Phoenicophorium borsigianum

Phyllanthus pervilleanus
Pisonia grandis
Pittosporum senacia
Planchonella obovata
Premna serratifolia
Psychotria pervillei
Pyrostria bibracteata
Rothmannia annae
Scaevola taccada
Sophora tomentosa
Suriana maritima
Syzygium grande
Tabernaemontana coffeoides
Tarenna sechellensis
Terminalia catappa
Thespesia populnea
Trema orientale
Verschaffeltia splendida
Wielandia elegans
Xylocarpus moluccensis

6
NIROX ESTATE (REFLECTION)

1. Scarlet River Lily (*Hesperantha coccinea*) | 2. Cape Water Lily (*Nymphaea nouchali* var. *caerulea*)
3. Hedgehog Sedge (*Cyperus congestus*)

Acalypha angustata
Acokanthera oppositifolia
Afrosciadium magalismontanum
Afrosolen sandersonii
Agapanthus campanulatus
Albuca glauca
Albuca setosa
Albuca virens subsp. *virens*
Alectra orobanchoides
Aloe davyana
Aloe marlothii
Aloe mutabilis
Aloe transvaalensis
Alsophila dregei
Ammocharis coranica
Antherotoma debilis
Apodytes dimidiata
Artemisia afra
Asclepias stellifera
Asparagus africanus var. *africanus*
Afroaster serrulatus
Athrixia elata
Barleria obtusa
Barleria pretoriensis
Berkheya carlinopsis
  subsp. *magalismontana*
Berkheya seminivea
Berkheya setifera
Berula repanda
Bonatea antennifera
Bonatea polypodantha
Bonatea porrecta
Boophone disticha
Buddleja salviifolia
Bulbine abyssinica
Callilepis leptophylla
Carissa bispinosa
Cassine burkeana
Cassinopsis ilicifolia
Celtis africana
Cephalaria zeyheriana
Ceropegia barberae
Chironia palustris
  subsp. *transvaalensis*
Chironia purpurascens
  subsp. *humilis*
Chlorophytum bowkeri
Chlorophytum cooperi
Clematis brachiata
Cliffortia linearifolia
Clutia pulchella var. *pulchella*
Coccinia adoensis

Coleus hadiensis
Coleus kirkii
Combretum erythrophyllum
Commelina africana
Cotyledon orbiculata
Crabbea cirsioides
Crassula setulosa
Crinum graminicola
Crocosmia aurea
Crossandra greenstockii
Cussonia paniculata subsp. *sinuata*
Cyanotis lapidosa
Cyanotis speciosa
Cycnium adonense
Cynanchum insipidum
Cynanchum viminale subsp. *viminale*
Cyperus ascocapensis
Cyperus congestus
Cyphia stenopetala
Cyphostemma lanigerum
Dicliptera eenii
Dierama mossii
Dimorphotheca spectabilis
Diospyros lycioides
Diospyros whyteana
Dipcadi viride
Disa woodii
Dovyalis zeyheri
Drosera burkeana
Entada elephantina
Erica woodii subsp. *woodii*
Eriosema burkei
Erythrina zeyheri
Euclea crispa subsp. *crispa*
Eucomis autumnalis subsp. *clavata*
Eulophia ovalis var. *bainesii*
Eulophia ovalis var. *ovalis*
Euphorbia schinzii
Ficus thonningii
Ficus ingens
Ficus salicifolia
Floscopa glomerata
Freesia grandiflora
Gazania krebsiana subsp. *serrulata*
Gerbera ambigua
Gerbera viridifolia
Gladiolus crassifolius
Gladiolus dalenii
Gladiolus elliotii
Gladiolus longicollis
  subsp. *platypetalus*
Gloriosa modesta

Gomphocarpus fruticosus
Grewia flava
Grewia occidentalis
Gunnera perpensa
Gymnosporia buxifolia
Gymnosporia heterophylla
Gymnosporia polyacanthus
  subsp. *polyacanthus*
Haemanthus humilis subsp. *hirsutus*
Halleria lucida
Haplocarpha scaposa
Helichrysum argyrosphaerum
Helichrysum cooperi
Hesperantha coccinea
Heteromorpha arborescens
  var. *abyssinica*
Hibiscus calyphyllus
Hilliardiella aristata
Hilliardiella elaeagnoides
Hypericum aethiopicum
  subsp. *sonderi*
Hypoestes forskaolii
Hypoxis argentea var. *argentea*
Hypoxis hemerocallidea
Ilex mitis
Ipomoea crassipes var. *crassipes*
Jasminum multipartitum
Kalanchoe rotundifolia
Kiggelaria africana
Kleinia barbertonica
Kniphofia ensifolia
Kniphofia porphyrantha
Lannea edulis
Lantana rugosa
Ledebouria cooperi
Ledebouria ovatifolia
  subsp. *ovatifolia*
Leonotis leonurus
Leucosidea sericea
Linum thunbergii
Macledium zeyheri
Maytenus albata
Maytenus undata
Melasma scabrum var. *scabrum*
Mentha longifolia
Mimusops zeyheri
Monsonia biflora
Moraea pallida
Moraea stricta
Moraea thomsonii
Myrica pilulifera
Myrica serrata

Nirox Estate (Reflection) PLANT LIST

Myrothamnus flabellifolius
Myrsine africana
Nymphaea nouchali var. *caerulea*
Nymphoides thunbergiana
Ocimum angustifolium
Olea europaea subsp. *cuspidata*
Orbea lutea subsp. *lutea*
Osyris lanceolata
Oxalis depressa
Parinari capensis subsp. *capensis*
Pavetta gardeniifolia var. *gardeniifolia*
Pavetta zeyheri subsp. *zeyheri*
Pavonia columella
Pelargonium luridum
Phylica paniculata
Pittosporum viridiflorum
Plumbago zeylanica

Populus spp.
Rhamnus prinoides
Rhoicissus tridentata
   subsp. *cuneifolia*
Riocreuxia polyantha
Rothmannia capensis
Rubus rigidus
Salix mucronata
Dracaena aethiopica
Scadoxus puniceus
Searsia discolor
Searsia lancea
Searsia pyroides
Secamone filiformis
Senegalia ataxacantha
Silene undulata
   subsp. *undulata*

Sphedamnocarpus pruriens
   subsp. *galphimiifolius*
Tarchonanthus camphoratus
Utricularia bisquamata
Vachellia karroo
Vachellia robusta
   subsp. *robusta*
Vachellia tortilis
Xerophyta retinervis
Xerophyta viscosa
Ximenia caffra var. *natalensis*
Xyris capensis
Xysmalobium undulatum
   var. *undulatum*
Zanthoxylum capense
Ziziphus mucronata
   subsp. *mucronata*

7
ARCADIA (THE PINES)

1. Reitz's Aloe (*Aloe reitzii*) | 2. Wild Grape (*Rhoicissus tridentata*) | 3. Feather Duster (*Clematis villosa* subsp. *villosa*)

The aloes at Arcadia (The Pines) comprise an outstanding, perhaps unique, collection of South African aloes and other African aloes, including species from Angola, Eritrea, Ethiopia, Kenya, Malawi, Mozambique, Nigeria, Somalia, Sudan, Tanzania and Zimbabwe, as well as Madagascar, Mauritius and the Middle East. Taxonomic revision of the genus *Aloe* in recent years has resulted in changes in some scientific names. The rambling aloes are now classified in the newly established genus *Aloiampelos* and the tree aloes in the new *Aloidendron*. The new genus *Aristaloe* contains only the one species listed below.

Aloe aculeata
Aloe acutissima
Aloe affinis
Aloe africana
Aloe albida
Aloe alooides
Aloe ammophila
Aloe andongensis
Aloe arborescens
Aloe bakeri
Aloe davyana
Aloe bellatula
Aloe betsileensis
Aloe bowiea
Aloe boylei
Aloe branddraaiensis
Aloe brevifolia
Aloe bulbillifera
Aloe burgersfortensis
Aloe cameronii
Aloe camperi
Aloe candelabrum
Aloe capitata
Aloe castanea
Aloe chabaudii
Aloe chortolirioides
Aloe chortolirioides var. *woolliana*
Aloe conifera
Aloe cooperi
Aloe cryptopoda
Aloe davyana
Aloe decurva
Aloe dewetii
Aloe dominella
Aloe dyeri
Aloe ecklonis
Aloe esculenta
Aloe ferox
Aloe flexilifolia
Aloe fosteri
Aloe fouriei

Aloe globuligemma
Aloe grandidentata
Aloe greatheadii
Aloe greenii
Aloe hardyi
Aloe haworthioides
Aloe hazeliana
Aloe hlangapies
Aloe hazeliana var. *howmanii*
Aloe humilis
Aloe integra
Aloe inyangensis
Aloe jacksonii
Aloe jucunda
Aloe juvenna
Aloe kamnelii
Aloe kedongensis
Aloe kniphofioides
Aloe komatiensis
Aloe kraussii
Aloe lateritia var. *graminicola*
Aloe lettyae
Aloe linearifolia
Aloe longibracteata
Aloe lutescens
Aloe macrocarpa
Aloe macrosiphon
Aloe maculata
Aloe maculata subsp. *ficksburgensis*
Aloe marlothii
Aloe mawii
Aloe megalacantha
Aloe microstigma subsp. *microstigma*
Aloe mudenensis
Aloe mutabilis
Aloe mzimbana
Aloe nubigena
Aloe palmiformis
Aloe parvibracteata
Aloe peglerae
Aloe petricola

Aloe petrophila
Aloe pictifolia
Aloe pluridens
Aloe pratensis
Aloe pretoriensis
Aloe prinslooi
Aloe pruinosa
Aloe reitzii
Aloe saundersiae
Aloe secundiflora
Aloe simii
Aloe sinkatana
Aloe spicata
Aloe striata
Aloe subacutissima
Aloe suffulta
Aloe suprafoliata
Aloe swynnertonii
Aloe tauri
Aloe thompsoniae
Aloe thorncroftii
Aloe tomentosa
Aloe tormentorii
Aloe torrei
Aloe transvaalensis
Aloe trichosantha
Aloe vanbalenii
Aloe vandermerwei
Aloe verecunda
Aloe vogtsii
Aloe vryheidensis
Aloe wickensii
Aloe zebrina
Aloiampelos ciliaris
Aloiampelos commixta
Aloiampelos gracilis
Aloiampelos juddii
Aloiampelos striatula
Aloiampelos tenuior
Aloidendron barberae
Aristaloe aristata

OTHER PLANT SPECIES

- *Adenia digitata*
- *Adenia fruticosa*
- *Adenia glauca*
- *Adenia spinosa*
- *Cephalophyllum alstonii*
- *Clematis brachiata x Clematis villosa subsp. villosa*
- *Cotyledon campanulata*
- *Cotyledon orbiculata*
- *Crassula natans*
- *Duvalia polita*
- *Euphorbia cooperi*
- *Euphorbia grandicornis*
- *Euphorbia grandidens*
- *Euphorbia griseola*
- *Euphorbia knobelii*
- *Euphorbia lydenburgensis*
- *Euphorbia monteiori*
- *Euphorbia pseudocactus*
- *Euphorbia pulvinata*
- *Euphorbia schubei*
- *Euphorbia sekukuniensis*
- *Gasteria acinacifolia*
- *Gasteria nitida* var. *armstrongii*
- *Gasteria nitida* var. *nitida*
- *Gasteria batesiana*
- *Gasteria baylissiana*
- *Gasteria brachyphylla* var. *brachyphylla*
- *Gasteria croucheri*
- *Gasteria excelsa*
- *Gasteria obliqua*
- *Gasteria pillansii* var. *ernesti-ruschii*
- *Gasteria rawlinsonii*
- *Haworthia angustifolia*
- *Haworthia arachnoidea*
- *Haworthia bolusii* var. *blackbeardiana*
- *Haworthia cooperi*
- *Haworthia cymbiformis*
- *Haworthiopsis attenuata*
- *Haworthiopsis coarctata*
- *Haworthiopsis fasciata*
- *Huernia pendula*
- *Huernia transvaalensis*
- *Huernia zebrina*
- *Jordaaniella spongiosa*
- *Kalanchoe rotundifolia*
- *Kalanchoe thyrsiflora*
- *Khadia acutipetala*
- *Lithops lesliei*
- *Mesembryanthemum cordifolium*
- *Monadenium lugardiae*
- *Mossia intervallaris*
- *Rhoicissus tridentata*
- *Stapelia gettliffei*
- *Stapelia gigantea*
- *Stapelia grandiflora*
- *Stapelia leendertziae*
- *Talinum caffrum*

SELECTED REFERENCES

Cane, J., *Civilising Grass: The Art of the Lawn on the South African Highveld*. Johannesburg: Wits University Press, 2019.

Coates Palgrave, M., *Keith Coates Palgrave Trees of Southern Africa*. Rev. 3rd ed. Cape Town: Struik Nature, 2002.

Curtis, O., et al., *Field Guide to Renosterveld of the Overberg*. Cape Town: Struik Nature, 2020.

Fagan, G., *Roses at the Cape of Good Hope*. Cape Town: Breestraat-Publikasies, 1988.

Fairbridge, D., *Gardens of South Africa*. Cape Town: Maskew Miller, 1934.

Greig, D., *Herbert Baker in South Africa*. Cape Town: Purnell, 1970.

Hobhouse, P., *The Story of Gardening: A Cultural History of Famous Gardens from around the World*. London: Pavilion, 2019.

Hunt, J.D., 'The British garden and the Grand Tour', *Studies in the History of Art* 25, 1989, pp. 333–351.

Hunt, J.D., *Gardens and the Picturesque: Studies in the History of Landscape Architecture*. Cambridge, MA: MIT Press, 1992.

Kirkby, D., *Stars, Blinks and Dots (and a Little Chutzpah)*. Johannesburg: Beyond the Vale Publishing, 2021.

Kirsten, K., *Gardens to Inspire*. Cape Town: Struik Lifestyle, 2013.

Kirsten, K., *Gardening with Keith Kirsten*. Rev. 4th ed. Cape Town: Struik Lifestyle, 2019.

Knoll, C., 'The garden of Inanda House', *The Urban Green File* 2(5), 1997.

Knoll, C., 'Saving the endangered endemics of Mauritius', *Environmental Management* 2(1), 2006, pp. 24–29.

McHarg, I.L., *Design with Nature*. New York: American Museum of Natural History, 1969.

Montero, M.I. and Marx, R.B., *Roberto Burle Marx: The Lyrical Landscape*. Oakland, CA: University of California Press, 2001.

Mucina, L. and Rutherford, M.C., eds, *The Vegetation of South Africa, Lesotho and Swaziland*. Pretoria: South African National Biodiversity Institute, 2006.

Murray, N., 'The imperial landscape at Cape Town's Gardens'. M.A. dissertation, University of Cape Town, 2001.

Oppenheimer, N. and Oppenheimer, S., *Brenthurst Garden: Working with Nature*. Johannesburg: Privately published, 2014.

Peres, E. and Zambani, A., *Creating Coromandel: Marco Zanuso in South Africa*. London: Artifice Press, 2022.

Pim, J., *Beauty is Necessary: Preservation or Creation of the Landscape*. Cape Town: Purnell, 1971.

Rebelo, T., *Proteas: A Field Guide to the Proteas of Southern Africa*. 2nd ed. Cape Town: Fernwood Press, 2001.

Richards, K., 'Profile on Patrick Watson', *Landscape SA*, November 2006.

Smith, A.H., *The Brenthurst Gardens*. Johannesburg: The Brenthurst Press, 1988.

Stoffberg, H., Hindes, C. and Müller, L., eds, *The South African Landscape Architecture Compendium – An Introduction and Retrospective Overview*. Pretoria: Unisa Press, 2012.

Taylor, G. and Cooper, G., *Gardens of Obsession: Eccentric and Extravagant Visions*. London: Seven Dials, 2000.

Van Eeden, J., 'The representation of mythical Africa at The Lost City: A critical analysis.' Ph.D. thesis, University of South Africa, 2000.

Viney, G., *Colonial Houses of South Africa*. 3rd ed. Cape Town: Fernwood Press, 2000.

Watson, F., Brown, L. and Proust, A., *Stellenberg: The Story of a Garden*. Cape Town: Quivertree Publications, 2013.

Watts, P., *Edna Walling and her Gardens*. 2nd ed. Balmain, Sydney: Florilegium, 1991.

Wiesmeyer, E., *Joane Pim: South Africa's Landscape Pioneer*. Pinegowrie, Johannesburg: The Horticultural Society, 2007.

Wolfaardt, C., 'Of mice and (wo)men: Disneyland and the cultural aesthetics of entertainment in the new South Africa', *Image and Text*, 1997, pp. 10–14. https://journals.co.za/doi/pdf/10.10520/AJA10201497_78 (Accessed 6 July 2022).